A GIFT FOR

_____

FROM

_____

HIS NAME IS

Jesus

The Promise of God's Love Fulfilled

MAX LUCADO

Thomas Nelson
Since 1798

NASHVILLE DALLAS MEXICO CITY RIO DE JANEIRO BEIJING

HIS NAME IS *Jesus*

Published in Nashville, Tennessee, by Thomas Nelson®. Thomas Nelson® is a registered trademark of Thomas Nelson, Inc.

Thomas Nelson, Inc. titles may be purchased in bulk for educational, business, fund-raising, or sales promotional use. For information, please e-mail SpecialMarkets@ThomasNelson.com.

Scripture references are from the following sources: The NEW KING JAMES VERSION (NKJV) ©1979, 1980, 1982, 1992, 2002 Thomas Nelson, Inc., Publisher. The Holy Bible, *New International Version* (NIV). Copyright ©1973, 1978, 1984, International Bible Society. Used by permission of Zondervan Bible Publishers. *The Message* (MSG), copyright © 1993, 1994, 1995, 1996, 2000, 2001, 2002. Used by permission of NavPress Publishing Group. *New American Standard Bible* (NASB), © 1960, 1977, 1995 by the Lockman Foundation. The *New Century Version®* (NCV). Copyright © 1987, 1988, 1991 by Thomas Nelson, Inc. All rights reserved. The Holy Bible, *New Living Translation* (NLT), copyright © 1996. Used by permission of Tyndale House Publishers, Inc., Wheaton, Illinois 60189. All rights reserved. The *Amplified Bible* (AMP). The Amplified New Testament, copyright © 1954, 1958, 1987 by the Lockman Foundation. *The Living Bible* (TLB), copyright © 1971 by Tyndale House Publishers, Wheaton, Illinois 60187. All rights reserved. The *Contemporary English Version* (CEV) © 1991 by the American Bible Society. Used by permission. The *Revised Standard Version* of the Bible (RSV), copyright © 1946, 1952, 1971 by the Division of Christian Education of the National Council of the Churches of Christ in the USA.

Compiled by Terri Gibbs
Editorial Supervision: Karen Hill, Executive Editor for Max Lucado
Development Editor: Lisa Stilwell
Design: Koechel Peterson & Associates, Inc., Minneapolis, MN

ISBN 13: 978-1-4041-8673-6
ISBN 10: 1-4041-8673-5

www.thomasnelson.com

Printed and bound in China

CONTENTS

JESUS WAS, AT ONCE, COMMON AND NOT; alternately normal and heroic. One minute blending in with the domino players in the park, the next commanding the hell out of madmen, disease out of the dying, and death out of the dead. Who was this man who spoke as easily with kids and fishermen as widows and waves? It is the question that has echoed down through the centuries to us today.

HIS STORY WAS EXTRAORDINARY. He called himself divine, yet allowed a minimum-wage Roman soldier to drive a nail into his wrist. He demanded purity, yet stood for the rights of a repentant whore. He called men to march, yet refused to allow them to call him King. He sent men into all the world, yet equipped them with only bended knees and memories of a resurrected carpenter.

WE CAN'T REGARD HIM AS SIMPLY A GOOD TEACHER. His claims are too outrageous to limit him to the company of Socrates or Aristotle. Nor can we categorize him as one of many prophets sent to reveal eternal truths. His own claims eliminate that possibility.

WHO IS HE?

Let's try to find out. Let's follow his sandal-prints. Let's sit on the cold, hard floor of the cave in which he was born. Let's smell the sawdust of the carpentry shop. Let's hear his sandals slap the hard trails of Galilee. Let's sigh as we touch the healed sores of the leper. Let's smile as we see his compassion with the woman at the well. Let's let our voices soar with the praises of the multitudes. Let's try to see him.

My prayer is that as you read this book Jesus will emerge from a wavy figure walking out of a desert mirage to become the touchable face of a best friend. My idea is simple. Let's look at some places he went and some people he touched. Join me on a quest for his "God-manness." You may be amazed.

More important, you may be changed.

MAX LUCADO

He stilled a storm with one command.

He raised the dead with one proclamation.

He rerouted the history of the world with one life.

HIS BIRTH

Jesus...

he could hold the universe

in his palm

but gave it up to float

in the womb of a maiden.

A Lowly Place of Birth

Joseph also went up from the town of Nazareth in Galilee to Judea, to Bethlehem the town of David, because he belonged to the house and line of David. He went there to register with Mary, who was pledged to be married to him and was expecting a child. While they were there, the time came for the baby to be born, and she gave birth to her firstborn, a son. She wrapped him in cloths and placed him in a manger, because there was no room for them in the inn.

LUKE 2:4–7 NIV

ONE'S IMAGINATION is kindled thinking about the conversation of the innkeeper and his family at the breakfast table. Did anyone mention the arrival of the young couple the night before? Did anyone ask about their welfare? Did anyone comment on the pregnancy of the girl on the donkey? Perhaps. Perhaps someone raised the subject. But, at best, it was raised, not discussed. There was nothing that novel about them. They were, possibly, one of several families turned away that night.

Besides, who had time to talk about them when there was so much excitement in the air? Augustus did the economy of Bethlehem a favor when he decreed that a census should be taken. Who could remember when such commerce had hit the village?

No, it is doubtful that anyone mentioned the couple's arrival or wondered about the condition of the girl. They were too busy. The day was upon them. The day's bread had to be made. The morning's chores had to be done. There was too much to do to imagine that the impossible had occurred.

God had entered the world as a baby. . . .

A more lowly place of birth could not exist.

Off to one side sit a group of shepherds. They sit silently on the floor; perhaps perplexed, perhaps in awe, no doubt in amazement. Their night watch had been interrupted by an explosion of light from heaven and a symphony of angels. God goes to those who have time to hear him—so on this cloudless night he went to simple shepherds.

Near the young mother sits the weary father. If anyone is dozing, he is. He can't remember the last time he sat down. And now that the excitement has subsided a bit, now that Mary and the baby are comfortable, he leans against the wall of the stable and feels his eyes grow heavy. He still hasn't figured it all out. The mystery of the event puzzles him. But he hasn't the energy to wrestle with the questions. What's important is that the baby is fine and that Mary is safe. As sleep comes, he remembers the name the angel told him to use . . . Jesus. "We will call him Jesus."

Wide awake is Mary. My, how young she looks! Her head rests on the soft leather of Joseph's saddle. The pain has been eclipsed by wonder. She looks into the face of the baby. Her son. Her Lord. His Majesty. At this point in history, the human being who best understands who God is and what he is doing is a teenage girl in a smelly stable. She can't take her eyes off him. Somehow Mary knows she is holding God.

He came, NOT AS A FLASH OF LIGHT

OR AS AN UNAPPROACHABLE CONQUEROR,

but as one whose first cries were heard

by a peasant girl

and a sleepy carpenter.

A Heavenly Interpretation

GOD TAPPED HUMANITY on its collective shoulder. "Pardon me," he said, and eternity interrupted time, divinity interrupted carnality, and heaven interrupted the earth in the form of a baby. Christianity was born in one big heavenly interruption. ✳ Just ask the Bethlehem shepherds. We know so little about these men. Their names? Their ages? How many were on duty that night? We don't know. But this much we can safely assume: They had no expectations of excitement. These are sheep they are watching. "That night, some shepherds were in the fields nearby watching their sheep" (LUKE 2:8 NCV). We count sheep to go to sleep! ✳ Besides, this is the night shift. Might as well watch paint dry. Shepherds watching sheep sleep? Saying that sentence is more exciting than doing their job. Their greatest challenge was staying awake! These men expected no excitement. ✳ Nor did they want any. Any excitement was bad excitement—wolves, mountain lions, poachers. Shepherds treasured the predictable.

They coveted the calm. Their singular aim was to be able to tell their wives, "Nothing happened last night." ❊ Just because they wanted a calm night, however, didn't mean they would get it. ❊ "Then an angel of the Lord stood before them. The glory of the Lord was shining around them, and they became very frightened" (LUKE 2:9 NCV). ❊ Change always brings fear before it brings faith. We always assume the worst before we look for the best. God interrupts our lives with something we've never seen, and rather than praise, we panic! We interpret the presence of a problem as the absence of God and scoot! ❊ Good thing the shepherds lingered. Otherwise they might have missed the next verse. ❊ "Today your Savior was born in the town of David. He is Christ, the Lord" (LUKE 2:11 NCV). *God Came Near*

IT WASN'T ENOUGH FOR THE SHEPHERDS TO SEE THE ANGELS. YOU'D THINK IT WOULD HAVE BEEN. Night sky shattered with light. Stillness erupting with song. Simple shepherds roused from their sleep and raised to their feet by a choir of angels: "Glory to God in the highest!" Never had these men seen such splendor.

But it wasn't enough to see the angels. The shepherds wanted to see the One who sent the angels. Since they wouldn't be satisfied until they saw him, you can trace the long line of Jesus-seekers to a person of the pasture who said, "Let's go . . . . Let's *see* . . . ." (LUKE 2:15, NCV, italics mine)

The Magi had the same desire. They wanted to see Jesus. Like the shepherds, they were not satisfied with what they saw in the night sky. Not that the star wasn't spectacular. Not that the star wasn't historical. To be a witness of the blazing orb was a privilege, but for the Magi, it wasn't enough. It wasn't enough to see the light over Bethlehem; they had to see the Light of Bethlehem. It was him they came to see.

Just Like Jesus

"SHE WILL BRING FORTH A SON,
AND YOU SHALL CALL HIS NAME JESUS,
FOR HE WILL SAVE HIS PEOPLE
FROM THEIR SINS."

MATTHEW 1:21 NKJV

HIS NAME IS...

Jesus

JESUS

In the four Gospels of the New Testament, it's his most common name—used almost six hundred times. And a common name it was. Jesus is the Greek form of Joshua, Jeshua, and Jehoshua—all familiar Old Testament names. When God chose the name his son would carry, he chose a human name. He chose a name so typical that it would appear two or three times on any given class roll.

He was touchable, approachable, reachable.

Those who walked with him remembered him not with a title or designation, but with a name—Jesus.

When God chose to reveal himself, he did so (surprise of surprises) through a human body. The tongue that called forth the dead was a human one. The hand that touched the leper had dirt under its nails. The feet upon which the woman wept were calloused and dusty. And his tears . . . oh, don't miss the tears . . . they came from a heart as broken as yours or mine ever has been.

So, people came to him. My, how they came to him! They came at night; they touched him as he walked down the street; they followed him around the sea; they invited him into their homes and placed their children at his feet. Why? Because he refused to be a statue in a cathedral or a priest in an elevated pulpit. He chose instead to be Jesus.

GOD CAME NEAR

BECAUSE HE IS LOVE . . .

If you were God, would you sleep on straw,
     nurse from a breast, and be clothed in a diaper?
     I wouldn't, but Christ did.

He went from commanding angels to sleeping in the straw.

From holding stars to clutching Mary's finger.

When he saw the size of the womb, he could have stopped.

When he saw how tiny his hand would be, how soft his voice would be,
     how hungry his tummy would be, he could have stopped.

At the first whiff of the stinky stable, at the first gust of cold air.

The first time he scraped his knee or blew his nose or tasted burnt bagels,
     he could have turned and walked out.

When he saw the dirt floor of his Nazareth house.

When Joseph gave him a chore to do.

When his fellow students were dozing off during the reading of the Torah, his Torah.

At any point Jesus could have said, "That's it! That's enough! I'm going home."
     But he didn't.

He didn't, because he is love.

A Love Worth Giving

Completely Human, Completely Divine

ANGELS WATCHED as Mary changed God's diaper. The universe watched with wonder as the Almighty learned to walk. Children played in the street with him. And had the synagogue leader in Nazareth known who was listening to his sermons . . .

Jesus may have had pimples. He may have been tone-deaf. Perhaps a girl down the street had a crush on him or vice versa. It could be that his knees were bony. One thing's for sure: He was, while completely divine, completely human.

For thirty-three years he would feel everything you and I have ever felt. He felt weak. He grew weary. He was afraid of failure. He was susceptible to wooing women. He got colds, burped, and had body odor. His feelings got hurt. His feet got tired. And his head ached.

To think of Jesus in such a light is—well, it seems almost irreverent, doesn't it? It's not something we like to do; it's uncomfortable. It is much easier to keep the humanity out of the incarnation. Clean the manure from around the manger. Wipe the sweat out of his eyes. Pretend he never snored or blew his nose or hit his thumb with a hammer. . . .

But don't do it. For heaven's sake, don't. Let him be as human as he intended to be. Let him into the mire and muck of our world. For only if we let him in can he pull us out.

GOD CAME NEAR

49

Christ became one of us.

AND HE DID SO TO REDEEM ALL OF US.

GROWING UP IN NAZARETH

THE CITY OF NAZARETH sits on a summit. Certainly no Nazarene boy could resist an occasional hike to the crest to look out over the valley beneath. Sitting six hundred feet above the level of the sea, the young Jesus could examine this world he had made. Mountain flowers in the spring. Cool sunsets. Pelicans winging their way along the streams of Kishon to the Sea of Galilee. Thyme-besprinkled turf at his feet. Fields and fig trees in the distance. Do you suppose moments here inspired these words later? "Observe how the lilies of the field grow" (MATTHEW 6:28 NASB) or "Look at the birds of the air" (MATTHEW 6:26 NASB). The words of Jesus the rabbi were born in the thoughts of Jesus the boy.

To the north of Nazareth lie the wood-crowned hills of Naphtali. Conspicuous on one of them was the village of Safed, known in the region as "the city set upon the hill." Was Jesus thinking of Safed when he said, "A city set on a hill cannot be hidden" (MATTHEW 5:14 NASB)?

The maker of yokes later explained, "My yoke is easy" (MATTHEW 11:30 NASB). The one who brushed his share of sawdust from his eyes would say, "Why do you look at the speck that is in your brother's eye, but do not notice the log that is in your own eye?" (MATTHEW 7:3 NASB).

"When Jesus entered public life he was about thirty years old" (LUKE 3:23 MSG). In order to enter public life, you have to leave private life. In order for Jesus to change the world, he had to say good-bye to his world.

He had to give Mary a kiss. Have a final meal in the kitchen, a final walk through the streets. Did he ascend one of the hills of Nazareth and think of the day he would ascend the hill near Jerusalem?

He knew what was going to happen. "God chose him for this purpose long before the world began" (1 PETER 1:20 NLT). Every ounce of suffering had been scripted—it just fell to him to play the part.

Not that he had to. Nazareth was a cozy town. Why not build a carpentry business? Keep his identity a secret? Return in the era of guillotines or electric chairs, and pass on the cross. To be forced to die is one thing, but to willingly take up your own cross is something else. . . .

The day he left Nazareth is the day he declared his devotion for you and me.

Next Door Savior

He *"made Himself of no reputation, taking the form
of a bondservant, and coming in the likeness of men.
And being found in appearance as a man,
He humbled Himself and became obedient to the point of death,
even the death of the cross"* (PHILIPPIANS 2:7–8 NKJV).

Christ abandoned his reputation. No one in Nazareth saluted him as the Son of God. He did not stand out in his elementary classroom photograph, demanded no glossy page in his high school annual. Friends knew him as a woodworker, not star hanger. His looks turned no heads; his position earned him no credit. In the great stoop we call Christmas, Jesus abandoned heavenly privileges and aproned earthly pains. "He gave up his place with God and made himself nothing" (PHILIPPIANS 2:7 NCV).

God hunts for those who will do likewise.

Cure for the Common Life

The greatest discovery

IN THE UNIVERSE IS THE GREATEST

LOVE IN THE UNIVERSE—

He Left the Carpentry Shop

THE HEAVY DOOR CREAKED on its hinges as he pushed it open. With a few strides he crossed the silent shop and opened the wooden shutters to a square shaft of sunshine that pierced the darkness, painting a box of daylight on the dirt floor.

He looked around the carpentry shop. He stood a moment in the refuge of the little room that housed so many sweet memories. He balanced the hammer in his hand. He ran his fingers across the sharp teeth of the saw. He stroked the smoothly worn wood of the sawhorse. He had come to say good-bye.

It was time for him to leave. He had heard something that made him know it was time to go. So he came one last time to smell the sawdust and lumber.

Life was peaceful here. Life was so . . . safe.

Here he had spent countless hours of contentment. On this dirt floor he had played as a toddler while his father worked. Here Joseph had taught him how to grip a hammer. And on this workbench he had built his first chair.

I wonder what he thought as he took one last look around the room. Perhaps he stood for a moment at the workbench looking at the tiny shadows cast by the chisel and shavings. Perhaps he listened as voices from the past filled the air.

I wonder if he hesitated. I wonder if his heart was torn. I wonder if he rolled a nail between his thumb and fingers, anticipating the pain. . . .

It must have been difficult to leave. After all, life as a carpenter wasn't bad. It wasn't bad at all. Business was good. The future was bright and his work was enjoyable. . . .

I wonder if he wanted to stay. "I could do a good job here in Nazareth. Settle down. Raise a family. Be a civic leader."

I wonder because I know he had already read the last chapter. He knew that the feet that would step out of the safe shadow of the carpentry shop would not rest until they'd been pierced and placed on a Roman cross.

You see, he didn't have to go. He had a choice. He could have stayed. He could have kept his mouth shut. He could have ignored the call or at least postponed it. And had he chosen to stay, who would've known? Who would have blamed him?

But his heart wouldn't let him. If there was hesitation on the part of his humanity, it was overcome by the compassion of his divinity. His divinity heard the voices. His divinity heard the hopeless cries of the poor, the bitter accusations of the abandoned, the dangling despair of those who are trying to save themselves.

And his divinity saw the faces. Some wrinkled. Some weeping. Some hidden behind veils. Some obscured by fear. Some earnest with searching. Some blank with boredom. From the face of Adam to the face of the infant born somewhere in the world as you read these words, he saw them all.

And you can be sure of one thing. Among the voices that found their way into that carpentry shop in Nazareth was your voice. Your silent prayers uttered on tear-stained pillows were heard before they were said. Your deepest questions about death and eternity. . . .

He left because of you.

God Came Near

28

The babe of Bethlehem.

Immanuel.

Remember the promise of the angel? "'Behold, the virgin shall be with child, and bear a Son, and they shall call His name Immanuel,' which is translated, 'God with us'" (MATTHEW 1:23 NKJV).

Immanuel. The name appears in the same Hebrew form as it did two thousand years ago. "Immanu" means "with us." "El" refers to Elohim, or God. Not an "above us God" or a "somewhere in the neighborhood God." He came as the "with us God." God with us.

Not "God with the rich" or "God with the religious." But God with us. All of us. Russians, Germans, Buddhists, Mormons, truck drivers and taxi drivers, librarians. God with us.

HIS MISSION

Jesus...

The man.

The bronzed Galilean who spoke
with such thunderous authority and
loved with such childlike humility.

HE COULD HAVE LIVED OVER US OR AWAY FROM US.

But he didn't.

HE LIVED AMONG US.

He became a friend of the sinner and brother of the poor.

Jesus Is Tempted in the Wilderness

JESUS ENTERED THE JORDAN RIVER a carpenter and exited a Messiah. With skin still moist with the water [of his baptism], he turned away from food and friends and entered the country of hyenas, lizards, and vultures. He was "led around by the Spirit in the wilderness for forty days, being tempted by the devil. And He ate nothing during those days, and when they had ended, He became hungry" (LUKE 4:1–2 NASB).

The wilderness was not a typical time for Jesus. Normalcy was left at the Jordan and would be rediscovered in Galilee. The wilderness was and is atypical. A dark parenthesis in the story of life. A fierce season of face-to-face encounters with the devil.

Jesus faced temptation for forty nights. Please note, he didn't face temptation for one day out of forty. Jesus was "in the wilderness for forty days, being tempted by the devil" (VV. 1–2). The battle wasn't limited to three questions. Jesus spent a month and ten days slugging it out with Satan. The wilderness is a long, lonely winter. . . .

Remember how Satan teased him? "If you are the Son of God . . ." (LUKE 4:3, 9 NCV).

Why would Satan say this? Because he knew what Christ had heard at the baptism. "This is My beloved Son, in whom I am well-pleased" (MATTHEW 3:17 NASB).

"Are you really God's Son?" Satan is asking. Then comes the dare—"Prove it!" Prove it by doing something:

"Tell this stone to become bread" (LUKE 4:3 NASB).

"If You worship before me, it shall all be Yours" (V. 7).

"Throw Yourself down from here" (V. 9).

What subtle seduction! Satan doesn't denounce God; he simply raises doubts about God. Is his work enough? Earthly works—like bread changing or temple jumping—are given equal billing with heavenly works. He attempts to shift, ever so gradually, our source of confidence away from God's promise and toward our performance.

Jesus doesn't bite the bait. No heavenly sign is requested. He doesn't solicit a lightning bolt; he simply quotes the Bible. Three temptations. Three declarations.

"It is written . . ." (V. 4 NCV).

"It is written . . ." (V. 8 NCV).

"It is said . . ." (V. 12 NASB).

Jesus' survival weapon of choice is Scripture. If the Bible was enough for his wilderness, shouldn't it be enough for ours? Don't miss the point here. Everything you and I need for desert survival is in the Book. We simply need to heed it.

The world has never known a heart so pure,
A CHARACTER SO FLAWLESS.

His spiritual hearing was so keen he never missed a heavenly whisper.

His mercy so abundant he never missed a chance to forgive.

No lie left his lips, no distraction marred his vision.

He touched when others recoiled.
He endured when others quit.

Just Like Jesus

The life of Jesus Christ

IS A MESSAGE OF HOPE,

a message of mercy,

a message of life in a dark world.

JESUS' DISCIPLES FOLLOW HIM

"RABBI," John and Andrew asked, "where are you staying?" (JOHN 1:38 NCV). ❋ Pretty bold request. They didn't ask Jesus to give them a minute or an opinion or a message or a miracle. They asked for his address. They wanted to hang out with him. They wanted to know him. They wanted to know what caused his head to turn and his heart to burn and his soul to yearn. They wanted to study his eyes and follow his steps. . . . They wanted to know what made him laugh and if he ever got tired. And most of all, they wanted to know, *Could Jesus be who John said he was—and if he is, what on earth is God doing on the earth?* You can't answer such a question by talking to his cousin [John]; you've got to talk to the man himself. ❋ Jesus' answer to the disciples? "Come and see" (JOHN 1:39 NCV). ❋ They wanted more than salvation. They wanted the Savior. They wanted to see Jesus.

Just Like Jesus

He went to great pains to be as human as the guy down the street.
    He didn't need to study,
        but still went to the synagogue.

He had no need for income,
        but still worked in the workshop.

He had known the fellowship of angels and heard the harps of heaven,
        yet still went to parties thrown by tax collectors.

And upon his shoulders rested the challenge of redeeming creation,
        but he still took time to walk ninety miles
        from Jericho to Cana to go to a wedding.

A Wedding in Cana

PICTURE SIX MEN WALKING on a narrow road. The gold dawn explodes behind them, stretching shadows ahead. Early morning chill has robes snugly sashed. Grass sparkles with diamonds of dew.

The men's faces are eager, but common. Their leader is confident, but unknown. They call him Rabbi; he looks more like a laborer. And well he should, for he's spent far more time building than teaching. But this week the teaching has begun.

Where are they going? To the temple to worship? To the synagogue to teach? To the hills to pray? They haven't been told. . . .

Maybe it was Andrew who asked it. Perhaps Peter. Could be that all approached Jesus. But I wager that at some point in the journey, the disciples expressed their assumptions.

"So Rabbi, where are you taking us? To the desert?"

"No," opines another, "he's taking us to the temple."

"To the temple?" challenges a third. "We're on our way to the Gentiles!"

Then a chorus of confusion breaks out and ends only when Jesus lifts his hand and says softly, "We're on our way to a wedding."

Silence. John and Andrew look at each other. "A wedding?" they say. "John the Baptist would have never gone to a wedding. Why, there is drinking and laughter and dancing . . . ."

"WHY WOULD WE GO TO A WEDDING?"

Good question. Why would Jesus, on his first journey, take his followers to a party? Didn't they have work to do? Didn't he have principles to teach? Wasn't his time limited? How could a wedding fit with his purpose on earth?

Why did Jesus go to the wedding?

The answer? It's found in the second verse of John 2. "Jesus and his followers were also invited to the wedding" (NCV).

Jesus wasn't invited because he was a celebrity. He wasn't one yet. The invitation wasn't motivated by his miracles. He'd yet to perform any. Why did they invite him?

I suppose they liked him.

Big deal? I think so. I think it's significant that common folk in a little town enjoyed being with Jesus. I think it's noteworthy that the Almighty didn't act high and mighty. . . .

There is no hint that he ever used his heavenly status for personal gain. Ever. You just don't get the impression that his neighbors grew sick of his haughtiness and asked, "Well, who do you think made you God?"

His faith made him likable.

The Miracle of Wine at the Wedding

MARY WAS FACING A DILEMMA. The wedding was moving. The guests were celebrating . . . but the wine was gone. Back then, wine was to a wedding what cake is to a wedding today. . . . To offer wine was to show respect to your guests. Not to offer wine at a wedding was an insult. . . .

Note how Mary reacted. Her solution poses a practical plan for untangling life's knots. "They have no more wine," she told Jesus (JOHN 2:3 NCV).

Note the sequence of events in the next verse: "Jesus said to the servants, 'Fill the jars with water.' So they filled the jars to the top. Then he said to them, 'Now take some out and give it to the master of the feast.' So they took the water to the master. When he tasted it, the water had become wine" (JOHN 2:7–9 NCV).

Did you see the sequence? First the jars were filled with water. Then Jesus instructed the servants to take the water (not the wine) to the master.

Note, the water became wine after they had obeyed, not before.

Next time you face a common calamity, follow the example of Mary at the wineless wedding:

Identify the problem. *(You'll half-solve it.)*

Present it to Jesus. *(He's happy to help.)*

Do what he says. *(No matter how crazy.)*

God, motivated by love and directed by divinity,

SURPRISED EVERYONE.

HE BECAME A MAN.

In an untouchable mystery, he disguised himself as a carpenter

and lived in a dusty Judaean village.

Determined to prove his love for his creation,

he walked incognito through his own world.

His callused hands touched wounds and his compassionate words touched hearts.

He became one of us.

NO WONDER THEY CALL HIM THE SAVIOR

Now it happened that while the crowd was pressing around Him and listening to the word of God,
He was standing by the lake of Gennesaret; and He saw two boats lying at the edge of the lake;
but the fishermen had gotten out of them and were washing their nets. And He got into one of the boats,
which was Simon's, and asked him to put out a little way from the land. And He sat down and began
teaching the   from the boat. When He had finished speaking, He said to Simon,
"Put out into the deep water and let down your nets for a catch."

LUKE 5:1–4 NASB

JESUS PREACHES AND PROVIDES FISH

Jesus needs a boat; Peter provides one. Jesus preaches; Peter is content to listen. Jesus suggests a midmorning fishing trip, however, and Peter gives him a look. The it's-too-late look. He runs his fingers through his hair and sighs, "Master, we worked hard all night and caught nothing" (V. 5). Can you feel Peter's futility?

All night the boat floated fishless on the black sheet of the sea. Lanterns of distant vessels bounced like fireflies. The men swung their nets and filled the air with the percussion of their trade.

SWISH, SLAP . . . SILENCE.

SWISH, SLAP . . . SILENCE.

Oh, the thoughts Peter might have had. I'm tired. Bone tired. I want a meal and a bed, not a fishing trip. Am I his tour guide? Besides, half of Galilee is watching. I feel like a loser already. Now he wants to put on a midmorning fishing exhibition? You can't catch fish in the morning. Count me out.

Whatever thoughts Peter had were distilled to one phrase: "We worked hard all night and caught nothing" (V. 5).

Still he replies, "I will do as You say and let down the nets" (V. 5).

Peter shows no excitement. He feels none. Now he has to unfold the nets, pull out the oars, and convince James and John to postpone their rest. He has to work. If faith is measured in seeds, his is an angstrom. Inspired? No. But obedient? Admirably. And an angstrom of obedience is all Jesus wants.

"Put out into the deep water," the God-man instructs.

Why the deep water? You suppose Jesus knew something Peter didn't? . . . Finding fish is simple for the God who made them. To Jesus, the Sea of Galilee is a dollar-store fishbowl on a kitchen cabinet.

Peter gives the net a swish, lets it slap, and watches it disappear. Luke doesn't tell us what Peter did while he was waiting for the net to sink, so I will. (I'm glancing heavenward for lightning.)

I like to think that Peter, while holding the net, looks over his shoulder at Jesus. And I like to think that Jesus, knowing Peter is about to be half yanked into the water, starts to smile. A dash of white flashes beneath his whiskers. Jesus tries to hold it back, but can't.

"When they had done this, they enclosed a great quantity of fish, and their nets began to break; so they signaled to their partners in the other boat for them to come and help them. And they came and filled both of the boats, so that they began to sink" (VV. 6–7).

Peter's arm is yanked into the water. It's all he can do to hang on until the other guys can help. Within moments the four fishermen and the carpenter are up to their knees in flopping silver.

Peter lifts his eyes off the catch and onto the face of Christ. In that moment, for the first time, he sees Jesus. Not Jesus the Fish Finder. Not Jesus the Multitude Magnet. Not Jesus the Rabbi. Peter sees Jesus the Lord.

JESUS MAJORS IN

RESTORING HOPE

TO THE SOUL.

THE MAN COULDN'T WALK. He couldn't stand. His limbs were bent and his body twisted. A waist-high world walked past as he sat and watched. . . .

Whether he was born paralyzed or became paralyzed—the end result was the same: total dependence on others. Someone had to wash his face and bathe his body. He couldn't blow his nose or go on a walk. When he ran, it was in his dreams. . . .

When people looked at him, they didn't see the man; they saw a body in need of a miracle. That's not what Jesus saw, but that's what the people saw. And that's certainly what his friends saw. So they did what any of us would do for a friend. They tried to get him some help.

Word was out that a carpenter-turned-teacher-turned-wonder-worker was in town. And as the word got out, the people came. They came from every hole and hovel in Israel. They came like soldiers returning from battle—bandaged, crippled, sightless. The old with prune faces and toothless mouths. The young with deaf babies and broken hearts. Fathers with sons who couldn't speak. Wives with wombs that wouldn't bear fruit. The world, it seemed, had come to see if he was real or right or both.

By the time his friends arrived at the place, the house was full. People jammed the doorways. Kids sat in the windows. Others peeked over shoulders. How would this small band of friends ever attract Jesus' attention? They had to make a choice: Do we go in or give up? . . .

One said that he had an idea. The four huddled over the paralytic and listened to the plan to climb to the top of the house, cut through the roof, and lower their friend down with their sashes.

It was risky—they could fall. It was dangerous—he could fall. It was unorthodox—de-roofing is antisocial. It was intrusive—Jesus was busy. But it was their only chance to see Jesus. So they climbed to the roof.

Faith does those things. Faith does the unexpected. And faith gets God's attention. Look what Mark says: "When Jesus saw the faith of these people, he said to the paralyzed man, 'Young man, your sins are forgiven'" (MARK 2:5 NCV).

Finally, someone took him at his word! Four men had enough hope in him and love for their friend that they took a chance. The stretcher above was a sign from above—somebody believes! Someone was willing to risk embarrassment and injury for just a few moments with the Galilean.

Jesus was moved by the scene of faith.

The friends want . . . Jesus to give the man a new body so he can walk. Jesus gives grace so the man can live.

He Still Moves Stones

Jesus had KINDNESS *for the diseased*

and MERCY *for the rebellious*

and COURAGE *for the challenges.*

GOD WANTS YOU TO HAVE THE SAME.

A Dead Boy Is Raised to Life

TWO CROWDS.
ONE ENTERING THE CITY
AND ONE LEAVING.
*They couldn't be more diverse.
The group arriving buzzes with
laughter and conversation.
They follow Jesus. The group
leaving the city is solemn—
a herd of sadness hypnotized
by the requiem of death.
Above them rides the reason
for their grief—a cold body
on a wicker stretcher.*

The woman at the back of the procession is the mother. She has walked this trail before. It seems like just yesterday she buried the body of her husband. Her son walked with her then. Now she walks alone, quarantined in her sadness. She is the victim of this funeral. . . .

The followers of Jesus stop and step aside as the procession shadows by. The blanket of mourning muffles the laughter of the disciples. No one speaks. What could they say? They feel the same despair felt by the bystanders at any funeral. "Someday that will be me."

No one intervenes. What could they do? Their only choice is to stand and stare as the mourners shuffle past.

Jesus, however, knows what to say and what to do. When he sees the mother, his heart begins to break . . . and his lips begin to tighten. He glares at the angel of death that hovers over the body of the boy. "Not this time, Satan. This boy is mine."

At that moment the mother walks in front of him. Jesus speaks to her. "Don't cry." She stops and looks into this stranger's face. If she wasn't shocked by his presumption, you can bet some of the witnesses were.

Don't cry? Don't cry? What kind of request is that?

A request only God can make.

Jesus steps toward the bier and touches it. The pallbearers stop marching. The mourners cease moaning. As Jesus stares at the boy, the crowd is silent. . . .

"YOUNG MAN," his voice is calm, "COME BACK TO LIFE AGAIN."

The living stand motionless as the dead comes to life. Wooden fingers move. Gray-pale cheeks blush. The dead man sits up.

Luke's description of what happens next is captivating.

"Jesus gave him back to his mother" (LUKE 7:15 NIV).

How would you feel at a moment like this? What would you do? A stranger tells you not to weep as you look at your dead son. One who refuses to mourn in the midst of sorrow calls the devil's bluff, then shocks you with a call into the cavern of death. Suddenly what had been taken is returned. What had been stolen is retrieved. What you had given up, you are given back.

Jesus must have smiled as the two embraced. Stunned, the crowd breaks into cheers and applause. They hug each other and slap Jesus on the back. Someone proclaims the undeniable, "God has come to help his people" (LUKE 7:16 NIV).

WHEN HANDS EXTENDED AND VOICES DEMANDED, JESUS RESPONDED WITH LOVE.

HE DID SO BECAUSE THE CODE WITHIN HIM DISARMED THE ALARM. THE CODE IS WORTH NOTING:

"People are precious."

MANY OF THOSE HE HEALED WOULD NEVER SAY "THANK YOU," BUT HE HEALED THEM ANYWAY.

MOST WOULD BE MORE CONCERNED WITH BEING HEALTHY THAN BEING HOLY,

BUT HE HEALED THEM ANYWAY. SOME OF THOSE WHO ASKED FOR BREAD TODAY WOULD CRY

FOR HIS BLOOD A FEW MONTHS LATER, BUT HE FED THEM ANYWAY.

WHAT DID JESUS KNOW THAT ALLOWED HIM TO DO WHAT HE DID?

WHAT INTERNAL CODE KEPT HIS CALM FROM ERUPTING INTO CHAOS? HE KNEW THE VALUE OF PEOPLE.

IN THE EYE OF THE STORM

Jesus Calms a Storm

Jesus and the disciples are in a boat crossing the Sea of Galilee. A storm arises suddenly and what was placid becomes violent—monstrous waves rise out of the sea and slap the boat. Mark describes it clearly: "A furious squall came up, and the waves broke over the boat, so that it was nearly swamped" (MARK 4:37 NIV). ❋ It's very important that you get an accurate picture, so I'm going to ask you to imagine yourself in the boat. It's a sturdy vessel, but no match for these ten-foot waves. It plunges nose first into the wall of water. The force of the waves dangerously tips the boat until the bow seems to be pointing straight at the sky, and just when you fear flipping over backwards, the vessel pitches forward into the valley of another wave. A dozen sets of hands join yours in clutching the mast. All of your shipmates have wet heads and wide eyes. You tune your ear for a calming voice, but all you hear are screams and prayers. All of a sudden it hits you—someone is missing. Where is Jesus? He's not at the mast. He's not grabbing the edge. Where is he? Then you hear something—a noise . . . a displaced sound . . . like someone is snoring. You turn and look, and there curled in the stern of the boat is Jesus, sleeping! ❋ You don't know whether to be amazed or angry, so you're both. How can he sleep at a time like this? Or as the disciples asked, "Teacher, don't you care if we drown?" (MARK 4:38 NIV).

DID JESUS CARE? Of course! He just had a different perspective. The very storm that made the disciples panic made him drowsy. What put fear in their eyes put him to sleep. The boat was a tomb to the followers and a cradle to Christ. How could he sleep through the storm? Simple, he was in charge of it.

"He got up, rebuked the wind and said to the waves, 'Quiet! Be still!' Then the wind died down and it was completely calm. He said to his disciples, 'Why are you so afraid? Do you still have no faith?'" (MARK 4:39–40 NIV).

Incredible. He doesn't chant a mantra or wave a wand. No angels are called, no help is needed. The raging water becomes a still sea, instantly. Immediate calm. Not a ripple. Not a drop. Not a gust. In a moment the sea goes from a churning torrent to a peaceful pond. The reaction of the disciples? Read it in verse 41: "They were in absolute awe, staggered. 'Who is this anyway?' they asked. 'Wind and sea at his beck and call!'" (MSG).

They'd never met a man like this. The waves were his subjects and the winds were his servants. And that was just the beginning of what his sea mates would witness. Before it was over, they would see fish jump into the boat, demons dive into pigs, cripples turn into dancers, and cadavers turn into living, breathing people.

WHEN JESUS SAYS HE WILL KEEP YOU SAFE,
HE MEANS IT.

Don't we need someone to trust

WHO IS BIGGER THAN WE ARE?

JESUS SAYS:

"I am that person. Trust me."

God meets daily needs daily

AND MIRACULOUSLY.

HE DID THEN, HE DOES STILL,

and he will for you.

Jesus Heals Jairus' Daughter

The crowd outside the house parts to let the father pass. They would on any day. He is the city leader. But they do this day because his daughter is dying. . . .

Jairus steps quickly down the path through the fishing village of Capernaum. The size of the following crowd increases with every person he passes. They know where Jairus goes. They know whom he seeks. Jairus goes to the shore to seek Jesus. As they near the water's edge, they spot the Teacher, encircled by a multitude. A citizen steps ahead to clear a trail, announcing the presence of the synagogue ruler. Villagers comply. The Red Sea of humanity parts, leaving a people-walled path. Jairus wastes no seconds. "When he saw Jesus, he fell to his knees, beside himself as he begged, 'My dear daughter is at death's door. Come and lay hands on her so she will get well and live.' Jesus went with him, the whole crowd tagging along, pushing and jostling him" (MARK 5:22–24 MSG).

Jesus' instant willingness moistens the eyes of Jairus. For the first time in a long time, a sun ray lands on the father's soul. He all but runs as he leads Jesus back to the path toward home. Jairus dares to believe he is moments from a miracle. . . .

People scatter out of the way and step in behind. Servants rush ahead to inform Jairus' wife. But then, just as suddenly as Jesus started, Jesus stops. Jairus, unaware, takes a dozen more steps before he realizes he's walking alone. The people stopped when Jesus did. And everyone is trying to make sense of Jesus' question: "Who touched my clothes?" (MARK 5:30 NIV). The sentence triggers a rush of activity. Heads turn toward each other; disciples respond to Christ. Someone moves back so someone else can come forward.

Jairus can't see who. And, quite frankly, he doesn't care who. Precious seconds are passing. His precious daughter is passing. . . .

Jairus feels a touch on his shoulder. He turns to look into the pale face of a sad servant, who tells him, "Your daughter is dead. Do not trouble the Teacher" (LUKE 8:49 NKJV). . . .

Jesus heard the servant's words. No one had to tell him about the girl's death. Though separated from Jairus, occupied with the case of the woman, encircled by pressing villagers, Jesus never took his ear off the girl's father. Jesus was listening the entire time. He heard. He cared. He cared enough to speak to Jairus's fear, to come to Jairus's home.

"Then He took the child by the hand, and said to her, 'Talitha, cumi,' which is translated, 'Little girl, I say to you, arise.' Immediately the girl arose and walked" (MARK 5:41–42 NKJV).

A pronouncement from the path would have worked. A declaration from afar would have awakened the girl's heart. But Jesus wanted to do more than raise the dead. He wanted to show that he not only cares but that he comes. He comes to all.

EVERY DAY DESERVES A CHANCE

A Woman Is Healed of a Bleeding Disorder

A large crowd followed Jesus and pushed very close around him. Among them was a woman who had been bleeding for twelve years. She had suffered very much from many doctors and had spent all the money she had, but instead of improving, she was getting worse.

MARK 5:24–26 NCV

A CHRONIC menstrual disorder. A perpetual issue of blood. Such a condition would be difficult for any woman of any era. But for a Jewess, nothing could be worse. No part of her life was left unaffected.

Sexually . . . she could not touch her husband.

Maternally . . . she could not bear children.

Domestically . . . anything she touched was considered unclean. No washing dishes. No sweeping floors.

Spiritually . . . she was not allowed to enter the temple.

She was physically exhausted and socially ostracized. . . . She awoke daily in a body that no one wanted. She is down to her last prayer. And on the day we encounter her, she's about to pray it.

By the time she gets to Jesus, he is surrounded by people. He's on his way to help the daughter of Jairus, the most important man in the community. What are the odds that he will interrupt an urgent mission with a high official to help the likes of her? Very few. But what are the odds that she will survive if she doesn't take a chance? Fewer still. So she takes a chance.

"If I can just touch his clothes," she thinks, "I will be healed" (V. 28).

Risky decision. To touch him, she will have to touch the people. If one of them recognizes her . . . hello rebuke, good-bye cure. But what choice does she have? She has no money, no clout, no friends, no solutions. All she has is a crazy hunch that Jesus can help and a high hope that he will. . . .

Her part in the healing was very small. All she did was extend her arm through the crowd.

"If only I can touch him."

What's important is not the form of the effort, but the fact of the effort. The fact is, she did something. She refused to settle for sickness another day and resolved to make a move. . . . And with that small, courageous gesture, she experienced Jesus' tender power. . . .

God honors radical, risk-taking faith.

HE STILL MOVES STONES

God has a peculiar passion for the forgotten.
HAVE YOU NOTICED?

See his hand on the festered skin of the leper?

See the face of the prostitute cupped in his hands?

Notice how he responds to the touch of the woman with the hemorrhage?

Over and over again God wants us to get the message:
He has a peculiar passion for the forgotten.
What society puts out, God puts in.
What the world writes off, God picks up.

AND THE ANGELS WERE SILENT

To the lonely, Jesus whispers,
"I'VE BEEN THERE."

To the discouraged,
Christ nods his head and sighs,
"I'VE BEEN THERE."

JESUS FEEDS FIVE THOUSAND PEOPLE

Following the disciples are five thousand men and their families. Jesus tries to get away from the crowd by crossing the sea, only to find the crowd waiting for him on the other side. . . . He wanted to spend time with just the disciples, but instead he got a crowd. He wanted time to think, but instead he had people to face.

He spends time teaching them, and then he turns to Philip and inquires, "Where can we buy enough bread for all these people to eat?" (JOHN 6:5 NCV). . . .

How does Philip respond? . . . He knows the problem, but he has no clue as to the solution. "We would all have to work a month to buy enough bread for each person to have only a little piece" (JOHN 6:7 NCV). . . .

Equally disturbing is the silence of the other disciples. Are they optimistic? Read their words, and see for yourself. "No one lives in this place, and it is already very late. Send the people away so they can go to the countryside and towns around here to buy themselves something to eat" (MARK 6:35–36 NCV).

COME ON, GUYS. HOW ABOUT A LITTLE FAITH? "You can feed them, Jesus. No challenge is too great for you. We've seen you heal the sick and raise the dead; we know you can feed the crowd."

But that's not what they said. If faith is a candle, those fellows were in the dark.

It never occurred to the disciples to turn the problem over to Jesus. Only Andrew had such a thought, but even his faith was small. "Here is a boy with five loaves of barley bread and two little fish, but that is not enough for so many people" (JOHN 6:9 NCV).

Andrew at least comes to Jesus with an idea. But he doesn't come with much faith. In fact, one would be hard pressed to find much faith on the hill that day. . . .

What does Jesus do? "Then Jesus took the loaves of bread, thanked God for them, and gave them to the people who were sitting there. He did the same with the fish, giving as much as the people wanted" (JOHN 6:11 NCV).

When the disciples didn't pray, Jesus prayed. When the disciples didn't see God, Jesus sought God. When the disciples were weak, Jesus was strong. When the disciples had no faith, Jesus had faith. He thanked God.

For what? The crowds? The pandemonium? The weariness? The faithless disciples? No, he thanked God for the basket of bread. He ignored the clouds and found the ray and thanked God for it.

A GENTLE THUNDER

Praying
ON A MOUNTAINSIDE

"He went up on a mountainside by himself to pray"

(MATTHEW 14:23 NIV).

What Jesus dreamed of doing and what he seemed able to do were separated by an impossible gulf. So Jesus prayed.

We don't know what he prayed about. But I have my guesses:

He prayed that eyes blinded by power could see God's truth.

He prayed that disciples dizzied by success could endure failure.

He prayed that leaders longing for power would follow him to a cross.

He prayed that people desiring bread for the body would hunger for bread for the soul.

He prayed for the impossible to happen.

IN THE EYE OF THE STORM

Jesus Calls Peter to Walk on Water

THE WINDS ROAR DOWN ONTO THE SEA OF GALILEE LIKE A HAWK ON A RAT. LIGHTNING ZIGZAGS ACROSS THE BLACK SKY. THE CLOUDS VIBRATE WITH THUNDER. THE RAIN TAPS, THEN POPS, THEN SLAPS AGAINST THE DECK OF THE BOAT UNTIL EVERYONE ABOARD IS SOAKED AND SHAKING. TEN-FOOT WAVES PICK THEM UP AND SLAM THEM DOWN AGAIN WITH BONE-JARRING FORCE.

These drenched men don't look like a team of apostles who are only a decade away from changing the world. . . . They look more like a handful of shivering sailors who are wondering if the next wave they ride will be their last.

And you can be sure of one thing. The one with the widest eyes is the one with the biggest biceps—Peter. He's seen these storms before. He's seen the wreckage and bloated bodies float to shore. He knows what the fury of wind and wave can do. And he knows that times like this are not times to make a name for yourself; they're times to get some help.

That is why, when he sees Jesus walking on the water toward the boat, he is the first to say, "Lord, if it's you . . . tell me to come to you on the water" (MATTHEW 14:28 NIV).

Now, some say this statement is a simple request for verification. Peter, they suggest, wants to prove that the one they see is really Jesus and not just anyone who might be on a stroll across a storm-tossed sea in the middle of the night. (You can't be too careful, you know.) . . .

I don't buy that. I don't think Peter is seeking clarification; I think he's trying to save his neck. He is aware of two facts: He's going down, and Jesus is staying up. And it doesn't take him too long to decide where he would rather be.

Perhaps a better interpretation of his request would be, "Jeeeeeeeesus. If that is you, then get me out of here!"

"Come on" is the invitation.

And Peter doesn't have to be told twice. . . . When faced with the alternative of sure death or possible life, Peter knows which one he wants.

The first few steps go well. But a few strides out onto the water, and he forgets to look to the One who got him there in the first place, and down he plunges. . . .

Peter, on the other hand, knows . . . better than to bite the hand that can save him. His response may lack class—it probably wouldn't get him on the cover of *Gentleman's Quarterly* or even *Sports Illustrated* —but it gets him out of some deep water:

"Help me!"

And since Peter would rather swallow pride than water, a hand comes through the rain and pulls him up.

The message is clear.

As long as Jesus is one of many options, he is no option. As long as you can carry your burdens alone, you don't need a burden bearer. . . .

But when you mourn, when you get to the point of sorrow for your sins, when you admit that you have no other option but to cast all your cares on him, and when there is truly no other name that you can call, then cast all your cares on him, for he is waiting in the midst of the storm.

THE APPLAUSE OF HEAVEN

PEOPLE LONGED FOR HIS COMPASSIONATE TOUCH:

parents carrying their children,

the poor bringing their fears,

the sinful shouldering their sorrow.

AND EACH WHO CAME
WAS TOUCHED.

And one touched was changed.

THE HANDS THAT HUNG THE STARS

IN THE HEAVENS

ALSO WIPED AWAY THE TEARS

OF THE WIDOW AND THE LEPER.

MAX LUCADO

When Jesus came down from the hill, great crowds followed him.

Then a man with a skin disease came to Jesus. The man bowed down before him and said, "Lord, you can heal me if you will."

Jesus reached out his hand and touched the man and said, "I will. Be healed!" And immediately the man was healed from his disease.

MATTHEW 8:1–3 NCV

Jesus Touched the Untouchables

I WONDER . . . about the man who felt Jesus' compassionate touch. He makes one appearance, has one request, and receives one touch. But that one touch changed his life forever. . . .

I wonder about this man because in New Testament times leprosy was the most dreaded disease. The condition rendered the body a mass of ulcers and decay. Fingers would curl and gnarl. Blotches of skin would discolor and stink. Certain types of leprosy would numb nerve endings, leading to a loss of fingers, toes, even a whole foot or hand. Leprosy was death by inches.

The social consequences were as severe as the physical. Considered contagious, the leper was quarantined, banished to a leper colony.

In Scripture the leper is symbolic of the ultimate outcast: infected by a condition he did not seek, rejected by those he knew, avoided by people he did not know, condemned to a future he could not bear. . . .

Jesus' touch did not heal the disease, you know. Matthew is careful to mention that it was the pronouncement and not the touch of Christ that cured the condition. . . .

The infection was banished by a word from Jesus.

The loneliness, however, was treated by a touch from Jesus.

Jesus touched the untouchables of the world.

JUST LIKE JESUS

A WOMAN CAUGHT IN SIN

It's dawn. . . .

*A rooster crows his
early morning recital.*

*A dog barks
to welcome the day.*

*And a young carpenter
speaks in the courtyard.*

JESUS SITS surrounded by a horseshoe of listeners. Some nod their heads in agreement and open their hearts in obedience. They have accepted the teacher as their teacher and are learning to accept him as their Lord. . . .

We don't know his topic that morning. Prayer, perhaps. Or maybe kindness or anxiety. But whatever it was, it was soon interrupted when people burst into the courtyard.

Determined, they erupt out of a narrow street and stomp toward Jesus. The listeners scramble to get out of the way. The mob is made up of religious leaders, the elders and deacons of their day. Respected and important men. And struggling to keep her balance on the crest of this angry wave is a scantily clad woman.

Only moments before she had been in bed with a man who was not her husband. Was this how she made her living? Maybe. Maybe not. Maybe her husband was gone, her heart was lonely, the stranger's touch was warm, and before she knew it, she had done it. We don't know.

But we do know that a door was jerked open and she was yanked from a bed. She barely had time to cover her body before she was dragged into the street by two men the age of her father. What thoughts raced through her mind as she scrambled to keep her feet? . . .

With holy strides, the mob storms toward the teacher. They throw the woman in his direction. She nearly falls.

"We found this woman in bed with a man!" cries the leader. "The law says to stone her. What do you say?"

Cocky with borrowed courage, they smirk as they watch the mouse go for the cheese.

The woman searches the faces, hungry for a compassionate glance. She finds none. Instead, she sees accusation. Squinty eyes. Tight lips. Gritted teeth. Stares that sentence without seeing.

Cold, stony hearts that condemn without feeling.

She looks down and sees the rocks in their hands—the rocks of righteousness intended to stone the lust out of her. The men squeeze them so tightly that their fingertips are white. They squeeze them as if the rocks were the throat of this preacher they hate. . . .

I wonder, did it weary him to see hearts that were stained, even discarded?

Jesus saw such a heart as he looked at this woman. Her feet were bare and muddy. Her arms hid her chest, and her hands clutched each other under her chin. And her heart, her heart was ragged, torn as much by her own guilt as by the mob's anger.

So, with the tenderness only a father can have, he set out to untie the knots and repair the holes.

He begins by diverting the crowd's attention. He draws on the ground. Everybody looks down. The woman feels relief as the eyes of the men look away from her.

The accusers are persistent. "Tell us, teacher! What do you want us to do with her?"

He could have asked why they didn't bring the man. The law indicted him as well. He could have asked why they were suddenly blowing the dust off an old command that had sat on the shelves for centuries. But he didn't.

He just raised his head and offered an invitation, "I guess if you've never made a mistake, then you have a right to stone this woman." He looked back down and began to draw on the earth again.

Someone cleared his throat as if to speak, but no one spoke. Feet shuffled. Eyes dropped. Then thud . . . thud . . . thud . . . rocks fell to the ground.

And they walked away. Beginning with the grayest beard and ending with the blackest, they turned and left. They came as one, but they left one by one.

Jesus told the woman to look up. "Is there no one to condemn you?" He smiled as she raised her head. . . .

Maybe she expected him to scold her. Perhaps she expected him to walk away from her. I'm not sure, but I do know this: What she got, she never expected. She got a promise and a commission.

The promise: "Then neither do I condemn you" (JOHN 8:11 NIV).

The commission: "Go and sin no more."

GO AND SIN NO MORE.

Jesus

Christ . . . points to the sparrow, the most inexpensive
bird of his day, and says, "Five sparrows are sold for only two pennies,
and God does not forget any of them. . . . You are worth
much more than many sparrows" (LUKE 12:6–7 NCV).

God remembers the small birds of the world.
We remember the eagles. We make bronze statues of the hawk.
We name our athletic teams after the falcons. But God notices
the sparrows. He makes time for the children and takes note of the lepers.
He offers the woman in adultery a second chance and the thief on the cross
a personal invitation. Christ is partial to the beat up and done in.

A LOVE WORTH GIVING

As [Jesus] passed by,
He saw a man
blind from birth.

JOHN 9:1 NASB

This man has never seen a sunrise. Can't tell purple from pink. The disciples fault the family tree. "Rabbi, who sinned, this man or his parents, that he would be born blind?" (V. 2).

Neither, the God-man replies. Trace this condition back to heaven. The reason the man was born sightless? So "the works of God might be displayed in him" (V. 3).

Talk about a thankless role. Selected to suffer. Some sing to God's glory. Others teach to God's glory. Who wants to be blind for God's glory? Which is tougher—the condition or discovering it was God's idea?

The cure proves to be as surprising as the cause. "[Jesus] spat on the ground, and made clay of the spittle, and applied the clay to his eyes" (V. 6).

The world abounds with paintings of the God-man: in the arms of Mary, in the Garden of Gethsemane, in the Upper Room, in the darkened tomb. Jesus touching. Jesus weeping, laughing, teaching . . . but I've never seen a painting of Jesus spitting.

Christ smacking his lips a time or two, gathering a mouth of saliva, working up a blob of drool, and letting it go. Down in the dirt. (Kids, next time your mother tells you not to spit, show her this passage.) Then he squats, stirs up a puddle of . . . I don't know, what would you call it?

Holy putty? Spit therapy? Saliva solution? Whatever the name, he places a fingerful in his palm, and then, as calmly as a painter spackles a hole in the wall, Jesus streaks mud-miracle on the blind man's eyes. "Go, wash in the pool of Siloam" (V. 7).

The beggar feels his way to the pool, splashes water on his mud-streaked face, and rubs away the clay. The result is the first chapter of Genesis, just for him. Light where there was darkness. Virgin eyes focus, fuzzy figures become human beings, and John receives the Understatement of the Bible Award when he writes: "He . . . came back seeing" (V. 7).

Come on, John! Running short of verbs? How about "he raced back seeing"? "He danced back seeing"? "He roared back whooping and hollering"?

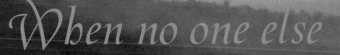

When no one else

WILL GIVE YOU THE TIME OF DAY,

JESUS WILL GIVE YOU

the words of eternity.

Lazarus Is Raised from Death

If Scripture boasted a list of the famous dead, Lazarus would be near the top. He lived in Bethany, a sleepy hamlet that sat a short walk from Jerusalem. Jesus spent a lot of time there. Maybe he liked the kitchen of Martha or the devotion of Mary. One thing is for sure: He considered Lazarus a friend. News of Lazarus' death prompts Jesus to say, "Our friend Lazarus has fallen asleep, but I am going there to wake him" (JOHN 11:11 NCV).

And now, four days after the funeral, Jesus has come calling. Literally calling, "Lazarus, come out!" Can we try to picture Lazarus as he hears those words? Heaven-sent Lazarus. Heaven-happy Lazarus. Four days into his measureless days. By now he's forming fast friendships with other saints. King David shows him the harps. Moses invites him over for tea and manna. Elijah and Elisha take him for a spin in the fiery chariot. Daniel has promised him a lion of a Bible story. He's on his way to hear it when a voice booms through the celestial city.

"Lazarus, come out!"

Everybody knows that voice. No one wonders, *Who was that?* Angels stop. Hosts of holy-city dwellers turn toward the boy from Bethany, and someone says, "Looks like you're going back for another tour of duty."

Lazarus doesn't question the call. Perfect understanding comes with a heavenly passport. He doesn't object. But had he done so, who could have faulted him? His heavenly body knows no fever. His future no fear. He indwells a city that is void of padlocks, prisons, and Prozac. With sin and death nonexistent, preachers, doctors, and lawyers are free to worship. Would anyone blame Lazarus for saying, "Do I have to go back?"

But he doesn't second-guess the command. Nor does anyone else. Return trips have been frequent of late. The daughter of the synagogue ruler. The boy from Nain. Now Lazarus from Bethany. Lazarus turns toward the rarely used exit door. The very one, I suppose, Jesus used some thirty earth years earlier. With a wave and within a wink, he's reunited with his body and waking up on a cold slab in a wall-hewn grave. The rock to the entrance has been moved, and Lazarus attempts to do the same. Mummy-wrapped, he stiffly sits up and walks out of the tomb with the grace of Frankenstein's monster.

People stare and wonder.

We read and may ask, "Why did Jesus let him die only to call him back?"

To show who runs the show. To trump the cemetery card. To display the unsquashable strength of the One who danced the Watusi on the neck of the devil, who stood face to clammy face with death and declared, "You call that a dead end? I call it an escalator."

"Lazarus, come out!"

Those words, incidentally, were only a warmup for the big day. He's preparing a worldwide grave evacuation. "Joe, come out!" "Maria, come out!" "Giuseppe, come out!" "Jacob, come out!" Grave after grave will empty. What happened to Lazarus will happen to us. Only our spirit-body reunion will occur in heaven, not Bethany Memorial Cemetery.

When this happens—when our perishable earthly bodies have been transformed into heavenly bodies that will never die—then at last the Scriptures will come true:

> "Death is swallowed up in victory.
> O death, where is your victory?
> O death, where is your sting?"

1 CORINTHIANS 15:54–55 NASB

"And he healed them"

is too short a phrase to describe
what must have been an astonishing sight.

Let your imagination go. Can you see the scene?

Can you see the blind husband seeing his wife for the first time?
His eyes gazing into her tear-filled ones like she was the queen of the morning?

Envision the man who had never walked, now walking!
Don't you know that he didn't want to sit down?
Don't you know that he ran and jumped and did a dance with the kids?

And the deaf woman who could now hear.
What was it like when she heard her child call her "Mamma" for the first time? . . .

I can picture a mom and dad standing
speechless before the Healer as they hold their newly healed baby.

I can envision a leper staring in awe at the One who took away his terror.

Thank you!

I can imagine throngs of people pushing and shoving.

Wanting to get close. Not to request anything or demand anything,

but just to say "thank you."

In the Eye of the Storm

HOW WIDE WAS HIS LOVE?

Wide enough for the whole world.

When Jesus and his followers were leaving Jericho,
a great many people followed him.
Two blind men sitting by the road heard that Jesus was going by,
so they shouted, "Lord, Son of David, have mercy on us!"

MATTHEW 20:29–30 NCV

TWO BLIND MEN BEG TO BE HEALED

"THE PEOPLE WARNED the blind men to be quiet, but they shouted even more, 'Lord, Son of David, have mercy on us!'

"Jesus stopped and said to the blind men, 'What do you want me to do for you?'

"They answered, 'Lord, we want to see.'

"Jesus . . . touched their eyes, and at once they could see. Then they followed Jesus" (MATTHEW 20:34 NCV).

Matthew doesn't tell us why the people refused to let the blind men get close to Jesus—but it's easy to figure it out. They want to protect him. He's on a mission, a critical mission. The future of Israel is at stake. He is an important man with a crucial task. He hasn't time for indigents on the side of the road.

Besides, look at them. Dirty. Loud. Obnoxious. Embarrassing. Don't they have any sense of propriety? Don't they have any dignity? These things must be handled in the proper procedure. First talk to Nathanael who talks to John who talks to Peter who then decides if the matter is worth troubling the Master or not.

But despite their sincerity, the disciples were wrong.

You see, in the eyes of those closest to Jesus, these blind men had no right to interfere with the Master. After all, he is on his way to Jerusalem. The Son of Man is going to establish the kingdom. He has no time to hear the needs of some blind beggars on the side of the road.

So, the people warned the blind men to be quiet.

They are a nuisance, these beggars. Look at the way they are dressed. Look at the way they act. Look at the way they cry for help. Jesus has more important things to do than to be bothered by such insignificant people.

Christ thought otherwise. Jesus "felt sorry for the blind men and touched their eyes, and at once they could see."

Jesus hears them in spite of the clamor. And of all the people, it is the blind who really see Jesus.

Something told these two beggars that God is more concerned with the right heart than he is the right clothes or procedure. Somehow they knew that what they lacked in method could be made up for in motive, so they called out at the top of their lungs. And they were heard.

God always hears those who seek him.

*"Come to me, all you who are weary and
burdened, and I will give you rest"*

MATTHEW 11:28 NIV.

COME TO ME. . . . The invitation is to come to him. *Why him?*

He offers the invitation as a penniless rabbi in an oppressed nation.
He has no political office, no connections with the authorities in Rome.
He hasn't written a bestseller or earned a diploma.

Yet, he dares to look into the leathery faces of farmers and tired faces
of housewives and offer rest. He looks into the disillusioned eyes of a preacher
or two from Jerusalem. He gazes into the cynical stare of a banker
and the hungry eyes of a bartender and makes this paradoxical promise:
"Take my yoke upon you and learn from me, for I am gentle and humble in heart,
and you will find rest for your souls" (MATTHEW 11:29 NIV).

The people came. They came out of the cul-de-sacs and office complexes
of their day. They brought him the burdens of their existence,
and he gave them not religion, not doctrine, not systems, but rest.

As a result, they called him Lord.
As a result, they called him Savior.

SIX HOURS ONE FRIDAY

Angry in the Temple

WHEN HE HAD ENTERED THE CITY on the back of a donkey, Jesus "went into the Temple. After he had looked at everything, since it was already late, he went out to Bethany with the twelve apostles" (MARK 11:11 NCV).

Did you catch that? The first place Jesus went when he arrived in Jerusalem was the temple. He'd just been paraded through the streets and treated like a king. It was Sunday, the first day of the Passover week. Hundreds of thousands of people packed the narrow stone streets. Rivers of pilgrims flooded the marketplace. Jesus elbowed his way through the sea of people as evening was about to fall. He walked into the temple area, looked around, and walked out.

Want to know what he saw? Then read what he did on Monday, the next morning when he returned.

Jesus went into the temple and threw out all the people who were buying and selling there. He turned over the tables of those who were exchanging different kinds of money, and he upset the benches of those who were selling doves. Jesus said to all the people there, "It is written in the Scriptures, 'My Temple will be called a house for prayer. . . . But you are changing God's House into a 'hideout for robbers'" (MARK 11:17 NCV).

What did he see? Hucksters. Faith peddlers. What lit the fire under Jesus' broiler? What was his first thought on Monday? People in the temple making a franchise out of the faith.

It was Passover week. The Passover was the highlight of the Jewish calendar. People came from all regions and many countries to be present for the celebration. Upon arriving they were obligated to meet two requirements.

FIRST, an animal sacrifice, usually a dove. The dove had to be perfect, without blem[ish]. The animal could be brought in from anywhere, but odds were that if you brought a sacrifice from another place, yours would be considered insufficient by the authorities in the temple. So, under the guise of keeping the sacrifice pure, the dove sellers sold doves—at their price.

SECOND, the people had to pay a tax, a temple tax. It was due every year. During Passover the tax had to be rendered in local currency. Knowing many foreigners would be in Jerusalem to pay the tax, moneychangers conveniently set up tables and offered to exchange the foreign money for local—for a modest fee, of course.

It's not difficult to see what angered Jesus. Pilgrims journeyed days to see God, to witness the holy, to worship His Majesty. But before they were taken into the presence of God, they were taken to the cleaners. What was promised and what was delivered were two different things. . . .

"I've had enough," was written all over the Messiah's face. In he stormed. Doves flapped and tables flew. People scampered and traders scattered.

This was not an impulsive show. This was not a temper tantrum. It was a deliberate act with an intentional message. Jesus had seen the moneychangers the day before. He went to sleep with pictures of this midway and its barkers in his memory. And when he woke up the next morning, knowing his days were drawing to a close, he chose to make a point: "You cash in on my people and you've got me to answer to." God will never hold guiltless those who exploit the privilege of worship.

Supper at Simon's House

A CLUSTER OF FRIENDS encircle Jesus. They are at the table. The city is Bethany and the house is Simon's.

He was known as Simon the leper. But not any longer. Now he is just Simon. We don't know when Jesus healed him. But we do know what he was like before Jesus healed him. Stooped shoulders. Fingerless hand. Scabbed arm and infected back draped in rags. A tattered wrap that hides all of the face except for two screaming white eyes.

But that was before Jesus' touch. Was Simon the one Jesus healed after he delivered the Sermon on the Mount? Was he the one in the ten who returned to say thank you? Was he one of the four thousand Jesus helped in Bethsaida? Or was he one of the nameless myriads the gospel writers didn't take time to mention?

We don't know. But we know he had Jesus and his disciples over for dinner. . . .

Simon didn't forget what Jesus had done. He couldn't forget. Where there had been a nub, there was now a finger for his daughter to hold. Where there had been ulcerous sores, there was now skin for his wife to stroke. And where there had been lonely hours in quarantine, there were now happy hours such as this—a house full of friends, a table full of food.

No, Simon didn't forget. Simon knew what it was like to stare death in the face. He knew what it was like to have no home to call your own, and he knew what it was like to be misunderstood. He wanted Jesus to know that if he ever needed a meal and a place to lay his head, there was one house in Bethany to which he could go.

MARY POURS PERFUME ON JESUS

"Now is the right time," she told herself.

It wasn't an act of impulse. She'd carried the large vial of perfume from her house to Simon's. It wasn't a spontaneous gesture. But it was an extravagant one. The perfume was worth a year's wages. Maybe the only thing of value she had. It wasn't a logical thing to do, but since when has love been led by logic? . . .

Mary stepped up behind Jesus and stood with the jar in her hand. Within a couple of moments every mouth was silent and every eye wide as they watched her nervous fingers remove the ornate cover.

Only Jesus was unaware of her presence. Just as he noticed everyone looking behind him, she began to pour. Over his head. Over his shoulders. Down his back. She would have poured herself out for him if she could.

The fragrance rushed through the room. Smells of cooked lamb and herbs were lost in the aroma of the sweet ointment.

"Wherever you go," the gesture spoke, "breathe the aroma and remember one who cares."

On his skin the fragrance of faith. In his clothing the balm of belief. Even as the soldiers divided his garments her gesture brought a bouquet into a cemetery.

The other disciples had mocked her extravagance. They thought it foolish. Ironic. Jesus had saved them from a sinking boat in a stormy sea. He'd enabled them to heal and preach. He'd brought focus into their fuzzy lives. They, the recipients of exorbitant love, chastised her generosity.

"Why waste that perfume? It could have been sold for a great deal of money and given to the poor," they smirk.

Don't miss Jesus' prompt defense of Mary. "Why are you troubling this woman? She did an excellent thing for me" (MATTHEW 26:10 NCV).

Jesus' message is just as powerful today as it was then. Don't miss it: "There is a time for risky love. There is a time for extravagant gestures. There is a time to pour out your affections on one you love. And when the time comes—seize it, don't miss it."

And the Angels Were Silent

It encircled the angels and starstruck the shepherds
in the Bethlehem pasture.

Jesus radiates it.

John beheld it.

Peter witnessed it on Transfiguration Hill.

Christ will return enthroned in it.

Heaven will be illuminated by it.

One glimpse, one taste, one sampling,
and your faith will never be the same . . .

Glory.

God's glory.

Every act of heaven reveals God's glory. Every act of Jesus did the same.

GLORY!

Mercy IS THE DEEPEST GESTURE *of kindness.*

The evening meal was being served, and the devil had already prompted Judas Iscariot,
son of Simon, to betray Jesus. Jesus knew that the Father had put all things under his power,
and that he had come from God and was returning to God; so he got up from the meal,
took off his outer clothing, . . . and began to wash his disciples' feet,
drying them with the towel that was wrapped around him.

JOHN 13:2–5 NIV

JESUS WASHES HIS DISCIPLES' FEET

IT HAS BEEN A LONG DAY. Jerusalem is packed with Passover guests, most of whom clamor for a glimpse of the Teacher. The spring sun is warm. The streets are dry. And the disciples are a long way from home. A splash of cool water would be refreshing.

The disciples enter [the room], one by one, and take their places around the table. On the wall hangs a towel, and on the floor sits a pitcher and a basin. Any one of the disciples could volunteer for the job, but not one does.

After a few moments, Jesus stands and removes his outer garment. He wraps a servant's girdle around his waist, takes up the basin, and kneels before one of the disciples. He unlaces a sandal and gently lifts the foot and places it in the basin, covers it with water, and begins to bathe it. One by one, one grimy foot after another, Jesus works his way down the row.

In Jesus' day the washing of feet was a task reserved not just for servants, but for the lowest of servants. . . . The servant at the bottom of the totem pole was expected to be the one on his knees with the towel and basin.

In this case the One with the towel and basin is the King of the universe. Hands that shaped the stars now wash away filth. Fingers that formed mountains now massage toes. And the One before whom all nations will one day kneel now kneels before his disciples. Hours before his own death, Jesus' concern is singular. He wants his disciples to know how much he loves them. . . .

You can be sure Jesus knows the future of these feet he is washing. These twenty-four feet will not spend the next day following their Master, defending his cause. These feet will dash for cover at the flash of a Roman sword. Only one pair of feet won't abandon him in the garden. . . . Judas won't even make it that far! He will abandon Jesus that very night at the table. . . .

What a passionate moment when Jesus silently lifts the feet of his betrayer and washes them in the basin.

Jesus knows what these men are about to do. He knows they are about to perform the vilest act of their lives. By morning they will bury their heads in shame and look down at their feet in disgust. And when they do, he wants them to remember how his knees knelt before them and he washed their feet. . . .

He forgave their sin before they even committed it. He offered mercy before they even sought it.

JUST LIKE JESUS

Content to be known as a carpenter.

HAPPY TO BE MISTAKEN FOR THE GARDENER.

HE SERVED HIS FOLLOWERS BY WASHING THEIR FEET.

HE SERVES US BY DOING THE SAME.

Each morning he gifts us with beauty.

Each Sunday he calls us to his table.

Each moment he dwells in our hearts.

HIS DEATH

Jesus...

The palm that held the universe

took the nail of a soldier.

G OD WAS NEVER MORE SOVEREIGN

than in the details

of the death of his Son.

The Sufferings of His Broken Heart

GO WITH ME FOR A MOMENT to witness what was perhaps the foggiest night in history. The scene is very simple; you'll recognize it quickly. A grove of twisted olive trees. Ground cluttered with large rocks. A low stone fence. A dark, dark night.

Now, look into the picture. Look closely through the shadowy foliage. See that person? See that solitary figure? What's he doing? Flat on the ground. Face stained with dirt and tears. Fists pounding the hard earth. Eyes wide with a stupor of fear. Hair matted with salty sweat. Is that blood on his forehead?

That's Jesus. Jesus in the Garden of Gethsemane.

Maybe you've seen the classic portrait of Christ in the garden. Kneeling beside a big rock. Snow-white robe. Hands peacefully folded in prayer. A look of serenity on his face. Halo over his head. A spotlight from heaven illuminating his golden-brown hair.

Now, I'm no artist, but I can tell you one thing. The man who painted that picture didn't use the Gospel of Mark as a pattern. When Mark wrote about that painful night, he used phrases like these: "Horror and dismay came over him," "My heart is ready to break with grief," and "He went a little forward and threw himself on the ground."

Does this look like the picture of a saintly Jesus resting in the palm of God? Hardly. Mark used black paint to describe this scene. We see an agonizing, straining, and struggling Jesus. We see a "man of sorrows" (ISAIAH 53:3 NASB). We see a man struggling with fear, wrestling with commitments, and yearning for relief.

We see Jesus in the fog of a broken heart.

The writer of Hebrews would later pen, "During the days of Jesus' life on earth, he offered up prayers and petitions with loud cries and tears to the one who could save him from death" (HEBREWS 5:7 NIV).

My, what a portrait! Jesus is in pain. Jesus is on the stage of fear. Jesus is cloaked, not in sainthood, but in humanity.

The next time the fog finds you, you might do well to remember Jesus in the garden. The next time you think that no one understands, reread the fourteenth chapter of Mark. The next time your self-pity convinces you that no one cares, pay a visit to Gethsemane. And the next time you wonder if God really perceives the pain that prevails on this dusty planet, listen to him pleading among the twisted trees.

The next time you are called to suffer, pay attention. It may be the closest you'll ever get to God. Watch closely. It could very well be that the hand that extends itself to lead you out of the fog is a pierced one.

JESUS BETRAYED BY JUDAS

WHEN BETRAYAL COMES, what do you do? Get out? Get angry? Get even? You have to deal with it some way. Let's see how Jesus dealt with it.

Begin by noticing how Jesus saw Judas. "Jesus answered, 'Friend, do what you came to do'" (MATTHEW 26:50 NCV).

Of all the names I would have chosen for Judas, it would not have been "friend." What Judas did to Jesus was grossly unfair. There is no indication that Jesus ever mistreated Judas. There is no clue that Judas was ever left out or neglected. When, during the Last Supper, Jesus told the disciples that his betrayer sat at the table, they didn't turn to one another and whisper, "It's Judas. Jesus told us he would do this."

They didn't whisper it because Jesus never said it. He had known it. He had known what Judas would do, but he treated the betrayer as if he were faithful.

It's even more unfair when you consider the betrayal was Judas' idea. The religious leaders didn't seek him; Judas sought them. "What will you pay me for giving Jesus to you?" he asked (MATTHEW 26:15 NCV). The betrayal would have been more palatable had Judas been propositioned by the leaders, but he wasn't. He propositioned them.

And Judas' method . . . again, why did it have to be a kiss? (MATTHEW 26:48–49).

And why did he have to call him "Teacher"? (MATTHEW 26:49). That's a title of respect. The incongruity of his words, deeds, and actions—I wouldn't have called Judas "friend."

But that is exactly what Jesus called him.

Why? Jesus could see something we can't. . . .

Jesus knew Judas had been seduced by a powerful foe. He was aware of the wiles of Satan's whispers (he had just heard them himself). He knew how hard it was for Judas to do what was right.

He didn't justify what Judas did. He didn't minimize the deed. Nor did he release Judas from his choice. But he did look eye to eye with his betrayer and try to understand.

As long as you hate your enemy, a jail door is closed and a prisoner is taken. But when you try to understand and release your foe from your hatred, then the prisoner is released and that prisoner is you.

AND THE ANGELS WERE SILENT

John tells us that "Judas came there with a group of soldiers and some guards from the leading priests and Pharisees" (JOHN 18:3 NCV). . . . ✲ I always had the impression that a handful of soldiers arrested Jesus. I was wrong. At minimum two hundred soldiers were dispatched to deal with a single carpenter and his eleven friends! ✲ Also present were "some guards." This was the temple police. They were assigned to guard the holiest place during the busiest time of the year. They must have been among Israel's finest. ✲ And then there was Judas. One of the inner circle. Not only had Satan recruited the Romans and the Jews, he had infiltrated the cabinet. Hell must have been rejoicing. There was no way Jesus could escape. Satan sealed every exit. His lieutenants anticipated every move, except one. ✲ Jesus had no desire to run. He had no intent of escape. He hadn't come to the garden to retreat. What they found among the trees was no coward; what they found was a conqueror.

ON THE EVE OF THE CROSS,

Jesus made his decision.

HE WOULD RATHER

go to hell for you

THAN GO TO HEAVEN WITHOUT YOU.

PETER DENIES KNOWING JESUS

Peter had bragged, "Everyone else may stumble . . .
but I will not" (MATTHEW 26:33 NCV). Yet he did. . . .

He stood and stepped out of hiding and followed the noise till he saw
the torch-lit jury in the courtyard of Caiaphas.

He stopped near a fire and warmed his hands. . . .
Other people near the fire recognized him. "You were with him," they had
challenged. "You were with the Nazarene." Three times people said it,
and each time Peter denied it. And each time Jesus heard it.

Please understand that the main character in this drama of denial is not Peter,
but Jesus. Jesus, who knows the hearts of all people, knew the denial of his friend.
Three times the salt of Peter's betrayal stung the wounds of the Messiah.

How do I know Jesus knew? Because of what he did. Then "the Lord turned
and looked straight at Peter" (LUKE 22:61 NIV). When the rooster crowed, Jesus turned.
His eyes searched for Peter and they found him. At that moment there were
no soldiers, no accusers, no priests. At that predawn moment in Jerusalem
there were only two people—Jesus and Peter.

Peter would never forget that look.

On Trial before Pilate

The most famous trial in history is about to begin.

Jesus

THE JUDGE IS SHORT and patrician with darting eyes and expensive clothes. His graying hair trimmed and face beardless. He is apprehensive, nervous about being thrust into a decision he can't avoid. Two soldiers lead him down the stone stairs of the fortress into the broad courtyard. Shafts of morning sunlight stretch across the stone floor.

As he enters, Syrian soldiers dressed in short togas yank themselves and their spears erect and stare straight ahead. The floor on which they stand is a mosaic of broad, brown, smooth rocks. On the floor are carved the games the soldiers play while awaiting the sentencing of the prisoner.

But in the presence of the procurator, they don't play.

A regal chair is placed on a landing five steps up from the floor. The magistrate ascends and takes his seat. The accused is brought into the room and placed below him. A covey of robed religious leaders follow, walk over to one side of the room, and stand.

Pilate looks at the lone figure. . . .

"Are you the king of the Jews?"

For the first time, Jesus lifts his eyes. He doesn't raise his head, but he lifts his eyes. He peers at the procurator from beneath his brow. Pilate is surprised at the tone in Jesus' voice.

"Those are your words."

Before Pilate can respond, the knot of Jewish leaders mock the accused from the side of the courtroom.

"See, he has no respect."

"He stirs the people!"

"He claims to be king!"

Pilate doesn't hear them. Those are your words. No defense. No explanation. No panic. The Galilean is looking at the floor again.

Something about this country rabbi appeals to Pilate. He's different from the bleeding hearts who cluster outside. He's not like the leaders with the chest-length beards who one minute boast of a sovereign God and the next beg for lower taxes. His eyes are not the fiery ones of the zealots who are such a pain to the *Pax Romana* he tries to keep. He's different, this upcountry Messiah. . . .

Pilate wants to let Jesus go. *Just give me a reason,* he thinks, almost aloud. *I'll set you free.*

His thoughts are interrupted by a tap on the shoulder. A messenger leans and whispers. Strange. Pilate's wife has sent word not to get involved in the case. Something about a dream she had.

Pilate walks back to his chair, sits, and stares at Jesus. "Even the gods are on your side?" he states with no explanation.

He has sat in this chair before. It's a curule seat: cobalt blue with thick, ornate legs. The traditional seat of decision. By sitting on it Pilate transforms any room or street into a courtroom. It is from here he renders decisions.

How many times has he sat here? How many stories has he heard? How many pleas has he received? How many wide eyes have stared at him, pleading for mercy, begging for acquittal?

But the eyes of this Nazarene are calm, silent. They don't scream. They don't dart. Pilate searches them for anxiety . . . for anger. He doesn't find it. What he finds makes him shift again.

He's not angry with me. He's not afraid . . . he seems to understand.

Pilate is correct in his observation. Jesus is not afraid. He is not angry. He is not on the verge of panic. For he is not surprised. Jesus knows his hour and the hour has come.

Pilate is correct in his curiosity. Where, if Jesus is a leader, are his followers? What, if he is the Messiah, does he intend to do? Why, if he is a teacher, are the religious leaders so angry at him?

Pilate is also correct in his question. "What should I do with Jesus, the one called the Christ?" (MATTHEW 27:22 NCV).

Perhaps you, like Pilate, are curious about this one called Jesus. You, like Pilate, are puzzled by his claims and stirred by his passions. . . .

What do you do with a man who calls himself the Savior, yet condemns systems? What do you do with a man who knows the place and time of his death, yet goes there anyway?

Pilate's question is yours. "What will I do with this man, Jesus?"

You have two choices.

You can reject him. That is an option. You can, as have many, decide that the idea of God's becoming a carpenter is too bizarre—and walk away.

Or you can accept him. You can journey with him. You can listen for his voice amid the hundreds of voices and follow him.

Christ lived the life we could not live

AND TOOK THE PUNISHMENT WE COULD NOT TAKE

to offer the hope we cannot resist.

Jesus

WHY?

WHY?

Jesus was angry enough to purge the temple,

   hungry enough to eat raw grain,

   distraught enough to weep in public,

   fun loving enough to be called a drunkard,

   winsome enough to attract kids,

   weary enough to sleep in a storm-bounced boat,

   poor enough to sleep on dirt and borrow a coin for a sermon illustration,

   radical enough to get kicked out of town,

   responsible enough to care for his mother,

   tempted enough to know the smell of Satan,

   and fearful enough to sweat blood.

WHY? Why would heaven's finest Son endure earth's toughest pain? So you would know that "he is able . . . to run to the cry of . . . those who are being tempted and tested and tried" (HEBREWS 2:18 AMP).

Whatever you are facing, he knows how you feel.

NEXT DOOR SAVIOR

He, who can dig the Grand Canyon

WITH HIS PINKIE,

THINKS YOU'RE WORTH

his death on Roman timber.

The Soldiers Wanted Jesus' Blood

The soldiers? *They wanted blood.*

So they scourged Jesus. The legionnaire's whip consisted of leather straps with lead balls on each end. His goal was singular: Beat the accused within an inch of his death and then stop. Thirty-nine lashes were allowed but seldom needed. A centurion monitored the prisoner's status. No doubt Jesus was near death when his hands were untied and he slumped to the ground.

The whipping was the first deed of the soldiers.

The crucifixion was the third. (No, I didn't skip the second. We'll get to that in a moment.) Though his back was ribboned with wounds, the soldiers loaded the crossbeam on Jesus' shoulders and marched him to the Place of a Skull and executed him.

We don't fault the soldiers for these two actions. After all, they were just following orders. But what's hard to understand is what they did in between. Here is Matthew's description:

"Jesus was beaten with whips and handed over to the soldiers to be crucified. The governor's soldiers took Jesus into the governor's palace, and they all gathered around him. They took off his clothes and put a red robe on him. Using thorny branches, they made a crown, put it on his head, and put a stick in his right hand. Then the soldiers bowed before Jesus and made fun of him, saying, "Hail, King of the Jews!" They spat on Jesus. Then they took his stick and began to beat him on the head. After they finished, the soldiers took off the robe and put his own clothes on him again. Then they led him away to be crucified" (MATTHEW 27:26–31 NCV).

The soldiers' assignment was simple: Take the Nazarene to the hill and kill him. But they had another idea. They wanted to have some fun first. Strong, rested, armed soldiers encircled an exhausted, nearly dead, Galilean carpenter and beat up on him. The scourging was commanded. The crucifixion was ordered. But who would draw pleasure out of spitting on a half-dead man?

Spitting isn't intended to hurt the body—it can't. Spitting is intended to degrade the soul, and it does. What were the soldiers doing? Were they not elevating themselves at the expense of another? They felt big by making Christ look small.

Allow the spit of the soldiers to symbolize the filth in our hearts. And then observe what Jesus does with our filth. He carries it to the cross.

Through the prophet he said, "I did not hide my face from mocking and spitting" (ISAIAH 50:6 NIV). Mingled with his blood and sweat was the essence of our sin.

God could have deemed otherwise. In God's plan, Jesus was offered wine for his throat, so why not a towel for his face? Simon carried the cross of Jesus, but he didn't mop the cheek of Jesus. Angels were a prayer away. Couldn't they have taken the spittle away?

They could have, but Jesus never commanded them to. For some reason, the One who chose the nails also chose the saliva. Along with the spear and the sponge of man, he bore the spit of man.

The sinless One took on the face of a sinner so that we sinners could take on the face of a saint.

He Chose the Nails

The Crown of Thorns

AN UNNAMED SOLDIER took branches—mature enough to bear thorns, nimble enough to bend—and wove them into a crown of mockery, a crown of thorns.

Throughout Scripture thorns symbolize, not sin, but the consequence of sin. Remember Eden? After Adam and Eve sinned, God cursed the land: "So I will put a curse on the ground. . . . The ground will produce thorns and weeds for you, and you will eat the plants of the field" (GENESIS 3:17–18 NCV). Brambles on the earth are the product of sin in the heart.

The fruit of sin is thorns—spiny, prickly, cutting thorns.

I emphasize the "point" of the thorns to suggest a point you may have never considered: If the fruit of sin is thorns, isn't the thorny crown on Christ's brow a picture of the fruit of our sin that pierced his heart?

What is the fruit of sin? Step into the briar patch of humanity and feel a few thistles. Shame. Fear. Disgrace. Discouragement. Anxiety. Haven't our hearts been caught in these brambles?

The heart of Jesus, however, had not. He had never been cut by the thorns of sin. What you and I face daily, he never knew. Anxiety? He never worried! Guilt? He was never guilty! Fear? He never left the presence of God! Jesus never knew the fruits of sin . . . until he became sin for us.

He Chose the Nails

Simon from Cyrene Carries Jesus' Cross

A man named Simon from Cyrene, the father of Alexander and Rufus, was coming from the fields to the city. The soldiers forced Simon to carry the cross for Jesus.

MARK 15:21 NCV

SIMON GRUMBLES under his breath. His patience is as scarce as space on the Jerusalem streets. He'd hoped for a peaceful Passover. The city is anything but quiet. Simon prefers his open fields. And now, to top it off, the Roman guards are clearing the path for some who-knows-which dignitary who'll march his soldiers and strut his stallion past the people.

"There he is!"

Simon's head and dozens of others turn. In an instant they know. This is no dignitary.

"It's a crucifixion," he hears someone whisper. Four soldiers. One criminal. Four spears. One cross. The inside corner of the cross saddles the convict's shoulders. Its base drags in the dirt. Its top teeters in the air. The condemned man steadies the cross the best he can but stumbles beneath its weight. He pushes himself to his feet and lurches forward before falling again. Simon can't see the man's face, only a head wreathed with thorny branches.

A sour-faced centurion grows more agitated with each diminishing step. He curses the criminal and the crowd.

"Hurry up!"

"Little hope of that," Simon says to himself.

The cross-bearer stops in front of Simon and heaves for air. Simon winces at what he sees. The beam rubbing against an already-raw back. Rivulets of crimson streaking the man's face. His mouth hangs open, both out of pain and out of breath.

"His name is Jesus," someone speaks softly.

"Move on!" commands the executioner.

But Jesus can't. His body leans and feet try, but he can't move. The beam begins to sway. Jesus tries to steady it, but can't. Like a just-cut tree, the cross begins to topple toward the crowd. Everyone steps back, except the farmer. Simon instinctively extends his strong hands and catches the cross.

Jesus falls face-first in the dirt and stays there. Simon pushes the cross back on its side. The centurion looks at the exhausted Christ and the bulky bystander and needs only a instant to make the decision. He presses the flat of his spear on Simon's shoulder.

"You! Take the cross!"

Simon dares to object. "Sir, I don't even know the man!"

"I don't care. Take up the cross!"

Simon growls, steps out of the crowd onto the street, and balances the timber against his shoulder, out of anonymity into history, and becomes the first in a line of millions who will take up the cross and follow Christ.

He did literally what God calls us to do figuratively: Take up the cross and follow Jesus. "If any of you want to be my followers, you must forget about yourself. You must take up your cross each day and follow me" (LUKE 9:23 CEV).

THE CROSS.

Strange that a tool of torture would

COME TO EMBODY A MOVEMENT OF HOPE.

THE SIGN ON CHRIST'S CROSS

"This is the King of the Jews."

A hand-painted, Roman-commissioned sign. . . .

Why is a sign placed over the head of Jesus?

Why are the words written in three languages?

Could it be that this piece of wood is a picture of God's devotion? A symbol of his passion to tell the world about his Son? . . .

Pilate had intended the sign to threaten and mock the Jews. But God had another purpose . . . Pilate was God's instrument for spreading the gospel.

Every passerby could read the sign, for every passerby could read Hebrew, Latin, or Greek—the three great languages of the ancient world. "Hebrew was the language of Israel, the language of religion; Latin the language of the Romans, the language of law and government; and Greek the language of Greece, the language of culture. Christ was declared king in them all" (McHugh and McHugh, *The Trial of Jesus*). God had a message for each. "Christ is king." The message was the same, but the languages were different. Since Jesus was a king for all people.

HE CHOSE THE NAILS

Two Thieves, Two Crosses

SKULL'S HILL—windswept and stony. The thief—gaunt and pale. . . .

His situation is pitiful. He's taking the last step down the spiral staircase of failure. One crime after another. One rejection after another. Lower and lower he descended until he reached the bottom—a crossbeam and three spikes.

He can't hide who he is. His only clothing is the cloak of his disgrace. No fancy jargon. No impressive résumé. No Sunday school awards. Just a naked history of failure.

He sees Jesus. . . .

He hears the jests and the insults and sees the man remain quiet. He sees the fresh blood on Jesus' cheeks, the crown of thorns scraping Jesus' scalp, and he hears the hoarse whisper, "Father, forgive them."

Why do they want him dead?

Slowly the thief's curiosity offsets the pain in his body. He momentarily forgets the nails rubbing against the raw bones of his wrists and the cramps in his calves.

He begins to feel a peculiar warmth in his heart: He begins to care; he begins to care about this peaceful martyr.

There's no anger in his eyes, only tears.

He looks at the huddle of soldiers throwing dice in the dirt, gambling for a ragged robe. He sees the sign above Jesus' head. It's painted with sarcasm: King of the Jews. . . .

All of a sudden, his thoughts are exploded by the accusations of the criminal on the other cross. He, too, has been studying Jesus, but studying through the blurred lens of cynicism.

> *"So you're the Messiah, are you? Prove it by saving yourself—*
> *and us, too, while you're at it!"* (LUKE 23:39 TLB).

It's an inexplicable dilemma—how two people can hear the same words and see the same Savior, and one see hope and the other see nothing but himself.

It was all the first criminal could take. Perhaps the crook who hurled the barb expected the other crook to take the cue and hurl a few of his own. But he didn't. No second verse was sung. What the bitter-tongued criminal did hear were words of defense.

> *"Don't you fear God?"*

When it seems that everyone has turned away, a crook places himself between Jesus and the accusers and speaks on his behalf.

> *"Don't you even fear God when you are dying? We deserve to die for our evil*
> *deeds, but this man hasn't done one thing wrong."* (LUKE 23:40 TLB).

The soldiers look up. The priests cease chattering. Mary wipes her tears and raises her eyes. No one had even noticed the fellow, but now everyone looks at him.

Perhaps even Jesus looks at him. Perhaps he turns to see the one who had spoken when all others had remained silent. Perhaps he fights to focus his eyes on the one who offered this final gesture of love he'd receive while alive. I wonder, did he smile as this sheep straggled into the fold?

For that, in effect, is exactly what the criminal is doing. He is stumbling to safety just as the gate is closing. Lodged in the thief's statement are the two facts that anyone needs to recognize in order to come to Jesus. Look at the phrase again. Do you see them?

"We are getting what we deserve. This man has done nothing wrong."

(LUKE 23:41 NIV)

We are guilty and he is innocent.

We are filthy and he is pure.

We are wrong and he is right.

He is not on that cross for his sins. He is there for ours.

And once the crook understands this, his request seems only natural. As he looks into the eyes of his last hope, he made the same request any Christian has made.

"Remember me when you come into your kingdom." (LUKE 23:42 NIV).

No stained-glass homilies. No excuses. Just a desperate plea for help.

At this point Jesus performs the greatest miracle of the cross. Greater than the earthquake. Greater than the tearing of the temple curtain. Greater than the darkness. Greater than the resurrected saints appearing on the streets.

He performs the miracle of forgiveness. A sin-soaked criminal is received by a blood-stained Savior.

"Today you will be with me in Paradise. This is a solemn promise."

(LUKE 23:43 TLB).

WHEN ASKED TO DESCRIBE

the width of his love,

Christ stretched one hand to the right

and the other to the left and had them nailed

in that position

so you would know HE DIED LOVING YOU.

He died loving you.

THE TALE OF THE CRUCIFIED CROOK

If anyone was ever worthless, this one was.
If any man ever deserved dying, this man probably did.
If any fellow was ever a loser, this fellow was at the top of the list.

Perhaps that is why Jesus chose him to show us
what he thinks of the human race.

Maybe this criminal had heard the Messiah speak. Maybe he had seen
him love the lowly. Maybe he had watched him dine with the punks,
pickpockets, and potmouths on the streets. Or maybe not.

Maybe the only thing he knew about this Messiah was what he now saw:
a beaten, slashed, nail-suspended preacher. His face crimson with blood,
his bones peeking through torn flesh, his lungs gasping for air.

Something, though, told him he had never been in better company. And
somehow he realized that even though all he had was prayer,
he had finally met the One to whom he should pray.

No Wonder They Call Him the Savior

Nails didn't hold God to a cross.

Love did.

"Father Forgive Them"

The dialogue that Friday morning was bitter.

From the onlookers, "Come down from the cross if you are the Son of God!"

From the religious leaders, "He saved others but he can't save himself."

From the soldiers, "If you are the king of the Jews, save yourself."

Bitter words. Acidic with sarcasm. Hateful. Irreverent. Wasn't it enough that he was being crucified? Wasn't it enough that he was being shamed as a criminal? Were the nails insufficient? Was the crown of thorns too soft? Had the flogging been too short?

For some, apparently so. . . .

Of all the scenes around the cross, this one angers me the most. What kind of people, I ask myself, would mock a dying man? Who would be so base as to pour the salt of scorn upon open wounds? How low and perverted to sneer at one who is laced with pain. . . .

The words thrown that day were meant to wound. And there is nothing more painful than words meant to hurt. . . .

If you have suffered or are suffering because of someone else's words, you'll be glad to know that there is a balm for this laceration. Meditate on these words from 1 Peter 2:23 (NIV):

"When they hurled their insults at him, he did not retaliate; when he suffered, he made no threats. Instead, he entrusted himself to him who judges justly."

Did you see what Jesus did not do? He did not retaliate. He did not bite back. He did not say, "I'll get you!" "Come on up here and say that to my face!" "Just wait until after the resurrection, buddy!" No, these statements were not found on Christ's lips.

Did you see what Jesus did do? He "entrusted himself to him who judges justly." Or said more simply, he left the judging to God. He did not take on the task of seeking revenge. He demanded no apology. He hired no bounty hunters and sent out no posse. He, to the astounding contrary, spoke on their defense. "Father, forgive them, for they do not know what they are doing" (LUKE 23:34 NIV). . . .

"THEY DON'T KNOW WHAT THEY ARE DOING."

And when you think about it, they didn't. They hadn't the faintest idea what they were doing. They were a stir-crazy mob, mad at something they couldn't see so they took it out on, of all people, God. But they didn't know what they were doing.

Yes, the dialogue that Friday morning was bitter. The verbal stones were meant to sting. How Jesus, with a body wracked with pain, eyes blinded by his own blood, and lungs yearning for air, could speak on behalf of some heartless thugs is beyond my comprehension. Never, never have I seen such love. If ever a person deserved a shot at revenge, Jesus did. But he didn't take it. Instead he died for them. How could he do it? I don't know. But I do know that all of a sudden my wounds seem very painless. My grudges and hard feelings are suddenly childish.

Sometimes I wonder if we don't see Christ's love as much in the people he tolerated as in the pain he endured.

Amazing Grace.

No Wonder They Call Him the Savior

The cross.

Can you turn any direction without seeing one? Perched atop a chapel. Carved into a graveyard headstone. Engraved in a ring or suspended on a chain. The cross is the universal symbol of Christianity. An odd choice, don't you think? Strange that a tool of torture would come to embody a movement of hope. The symbols of other faiths are more upbeat: the six-pointed star of David, the crescent moon of Islam, a lotus blossom for Buddhism. Yet a cross for Christianity? An instrument of execution? ☀ Why is the cross the symbol of our faith? To find the answer look no farther than the cross itself. Its design couldn't be simpler. One beam horizontal—the other vertical. One reaches out—like God's love. The other reaches up—as does God's holiness. One represents the width of his love; the other reflects the height of his holiness. The cross is the intersection. The cross is where God forgave his children without lowering his standards. ☀ How could he do this? In a sentence: God put our sin on his Son and punished it there. ☀ "God put the wrong on him who never did anything wrong, so we could be put right with God" (2 CORINTHIANS 5:21 MSG).   HE CHOSE THE NAILS

Jesus

JESUS SPENT OVER THREE DECADES

WADING THROUGH THE MUCK

AND MIRE OF OUR SIN

YET STILL SAW ENOUGH BEAUTY IN US

TO DIE FOR OUR MISTAKES.

JESUS ASKS JOHN TO CARE FOR HIS MOTHER

Mary is older now. The hair at her temples is gray. Wrinkles have replaced her youthful skin. Her hands are callused. She has raised a houseful of children. And now she beholds the crucifixion of her firstborn.

One wonders what memories she conjures up as she witnesses his torture. The long ride to Bethlehem, perhaps. A baby's bed made from cow's hay. Fugitives in Egypt. At home in Nazareth. Panic in Jerusalem. "I thought he was with you!" Carpentry lessons. Dinner table laughter.

And then the morning Jesus came in from the shop early, his eyes firmer, his voice more direct. He had heard the news. "John is preaching in the desert." Her son took off his nail apron, dusted off his hands, and with one last look said good-bye to his mother. They both knew it would never be the same again. In that last look they shared a secret, the full extent of which was too painful to say aloud.

Mary learned that day the heartache that comes from saying good-bye. From then on she was to love her son from a distance: on the edge of the crowd, outside of a packed house, on the shore of the sea. . . .

"Woman, behold your son!"

John fastened his arm around Mary a little tighter. Jesus was asking him to be the son that a mother needs and that in some ways he never was.

Jesus looked at Mary. His ache was from a pain far greater than that of the nails and thorns. In their silent glance they again shared a secret. And he said good-bye.

Thirsty on the Cross

THIS IS THE FINAL ACT of Jesus' life. In the concluding measure of his earthly composition, we hear the sounds of a thirsty man.

And through his thirst—through a sponge and a jar of cheap wine—he leaves a final appeal.

"You can trust me."

Jesus. Lips cracked and mouth of cotton. Throat so dry he couldn't swallow, and voice so hoarse he could scarcely speak. He is thirsty. To find the last time moisture touched these lips you need to rewind a dozen hours to the meal in the Upper Room. Since tasting that cup of wine, Jesus has been beaten, spat upon, bruised, and cut. He has been a cross-carrier and sin-bearer, and no liquid has salved his throat. He is thirsty.

Why doesn't he do something about it? Couldn't he? Did he not cause jugs of water to be jugs of wine? Did he not make a wall out of the Jordan River and two walls out of the Red Sea? Didn't he, with one word, banish the rain and calm the waves? Doesn't Scripture say that he "turned the desert into pools" (PSALM 107:35 NIV) and "the hard rock into springs" (PSALM 114:8 NIV)?

Did God not say, "I will pour water on him who is thirsty" (ISAIAH 44:3 NKJV)?

If so, why does Jesus endure thirst?

While we are asking this question, add a few more. Why did he grow weary in Samaria (JOHN 4:6), disturbed in Nazareth (MARK 6:6), and angry in the temple (JOHN 2:15)? Why was he sleepy in the boat on the Sea of Galilee (MARK 4:38), sad at the tomb of Lazarus (JOHN 11:35), and hungry in the wilderness (MATTHEW 4:2)?

Why? And why did he grow thirsty on the cross?

He didn't have to suffer thirst. At least, not to the level he did. Six hours earlier he'd been offered drink, but he refused it.

"They brought Jesus to the place called Golgotha (which means The Place of the Skull). Then they offered him wine mixed with myrrh, but *he did not take it.* And they crucified him. Dividing up his clothes, they cast lots to see what each would get" (MARK 15:22–24 NIV, italics mine).

Before the nail was pounded, a drink was offered. Mark says the wine was mixed with myrrh. Matthew described it as wine mixed with gall. Both myrrh and gall contain sedative properties that numb the senses. But Jesus refused them. He refused to be stupefied by the drugs, opting instead to feel the full force of his suffering.

Why? Why did he endure all these feelings? Because he knew you would feel them too.

He knew you would be weary, disturbed, and angry. He knew you'd be sleepy, grief-stricken, and hungry. He knew you'd face pain. If not the pain of the body, the pain of the soul . . . pain too sharp for any drug. He knew you'd face thirst. If not a thirst for water, at least a thirst for truth, and the truth we glean from the image of a thirsty Christ is—he understands.

And because he understands, we can come to him.

JESUS' LAST WORDS ON THE CROSS

The hill is quiet now. Not still but quiet. For the first time all day there is no noise. The clamor began to subside when the darkness—that puzzling midday darkness—fell. Like water douses a fire, the shadows doused the ridicule. No more taunts. No more jokes. No more jesting. And, in time, no more mockers. One by one the onlookers turned and began the descent.

That is, all the onlookers except you and me. We did not leave. We came to learn. And so we lingered in the semidarkness and listened. We listened to the soldiers cursing, the passersby questioning, and the women weeping. But most of all, we listened to the trio of dying men groaning. Hoarse, guttural, thirsty groans. They groaned with each rolling of the head and each pivot of the legs.

But as the minutes became hours, these groans diminished. The three seemed dead. Were it not for the belabored breathing, you would have thought they were.

Then he screamed. As if someone had yanked his hair, the back of his head slammed against the sign that bore his name, and he screamed. Like a dagger cuts the curtain, his scream cut the dark. Standing as straight as the nails would permit, he cried as one calling for a lost friend, "Eloi!"

His voice was raspy, scratchy. Reflections of the torch flame danced in his wide eyes. "My God!"

Ignoring the volcano of erupting pain, he pushed upward until his shoulders were higher than his nailed hands. "Why have you forsaken me?"

The soldiers stared. The weeping of the women ceased. One of the Pharisees sneered sarcastically, "He's calling Elijah."

No one laughed.

He'd shouted a question to the heavens, and you half expected heaven to shout one in return.

And apparently it did. For the face of Jesus softened, and an afternoon dawn broke as he spoke a final time. "It is finished. Father, into your hands I commit my spirit."

As he gave his final breath, the earth gave a sudden stir. A rock rolled, and a soldier stumbled. Then, as suddenly as the silence was broken, the silence returned.

And now all is quiet. The mocking has ceased. There is no one to mock.

The soldiers are busy with the business of cleaning up the dead. Two men have come. Dressed well and meaning well, they are given the body of Jesus.

He Chose the Nails

A Cry of Victory

"IT IS FINISHED."

Stop and listen. Can you imagine the cry from the cross? The sky is dark. The other two victims are moaning. The jeering mouths are silent. Perhaps there is thunder. Perhaps there is weeping. Perhaps there is silence. Then Jesus draws in a deep breath, pushes his feet down on that Roman nail, and cries, "It is finished!"

What was finished?

The history-long plan of redeeming man was finished. The message of God to man was finished. The works done by Jesus as a man on earth were finished. The task of selecting and training ambassadors was finished. The job was finished. The song had been sung. The blood had been poured. The sacrifice had been made. The sting of death had been removed. It was over.

A cry of defeat? Hardly. Had his hands not been fastened down I dare say that a triumphant fist would have punched the dark sky. No, this is no cry of despair. It is a cry of completion. A cry of victory. A cry of fulfillment. Yes, even a cry of relief.

It's over.

An angel sighs. A star wipes away a tear.

"TAKE ME HOME."

Yes, take him home.
Take this prince to his king.
Take this son to his father.
Take this pilgrim to his home.
(He deserves a rest.)

"TAKE ME HOME."

Come ten thousand angels!
Come and take this wounded troubadour to
the cradle of his Father's arms!

Farewell manger's infant.
Bless you holy ambassador.
Go Home death slayer.
Rest well sweet soldier.

The battle is over.

It is finished?

How could Jesus say he was finished?

There were still the hungry to feed, the sick to heal,

the untaught to instruct, and the unloved to love.

How could he say he was finished?

Simple. He had completed his designated task.

His commission was fulfilled. The painter could set aside his brush,

the sculptor lay down his chisel, the writer put away his pen.

The job was done.

JUST LIKE JESUS

Do you feel a need for affirmation?

You need only pause at the base of the cross
and be reminded of this:

*The maker of the stars
would rather die for you
than live without you.*

And that is a fact.

Jesus

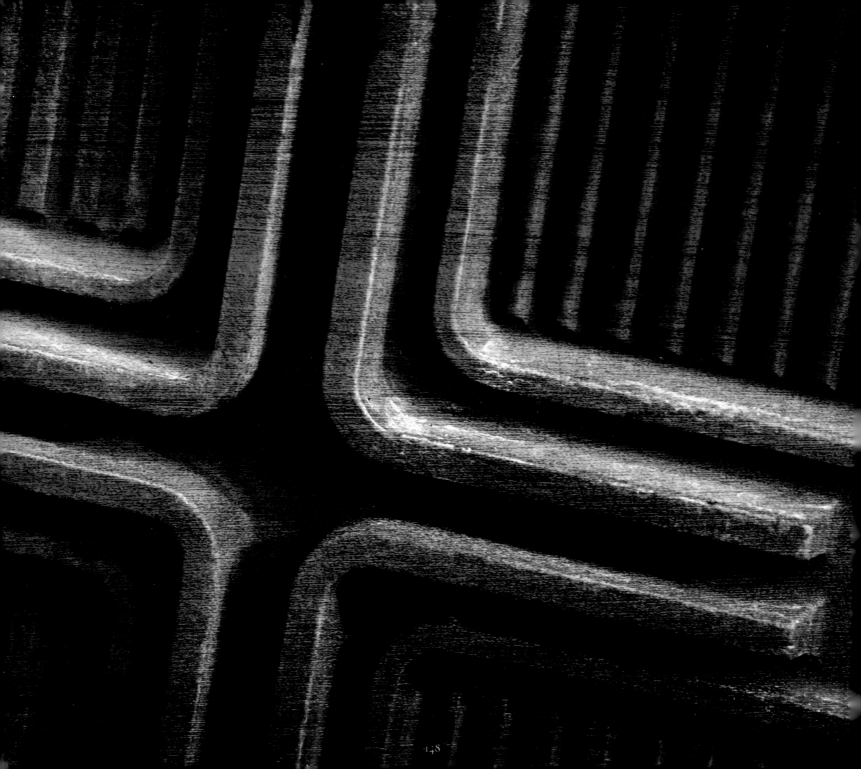

The Centurion at the Foot of the Cross

The centurion was no stranger to finality. Over the years he'd grown callous to the screams of the crucified. He'd mastered the art of numbing his heart. But this crucifixion plagued him.

THE DAY BEGAN as had a hundred others—dreadfully. It was bad enough to be in Judea, but it was hell to spend hot afternoons on a rocky hill supervising the death of pickpockets and rabble-rousers. Half the crowd taunted, half cried. The soldiers griped. The priests bossed. It was a thankless job in a strange land. He was ready for the day to be over before it began.

He was curious at the attention given to the flat-footed peasant. He smiled as he read the sign that would go on the cross. The condemned looked like anything but a king. His face was lumpy and bruised. His back arched slightly and his eyes faced downward. "Some harmless hick," mused the centurion. "What could he have done?"

Then Jesus raised his head. He wasn't angry. He wasn't uneasy. His eyes were strangely calm as they stared from behind the bloody mask. He looked at those who knew him—moving deliberately from face to face as if he had a word for each.

For just a moment he looked at the centurion—for a second the Roman looked into the purest eyes he'd ever seen. He didn't know what the look meant. But the look made him swallow and his stomach feel empty. As he watched the soldier grab the Nazarene and yank him to the ground, something told him this was not going to be a normal day.

As the hours wore on, the centurion found himself looking more and more at the one on the center cross. He didn't know what to do with the Nazarene's silence. He didn't know what to do with his kindness.

But most of all, he was perplexed by the darkness. He didn't know what to do with the black sky in midafternoon. No one could explain it. . . . No one even tried. One minute the sun, the next the darkness. One minute the heat, the next a chilly breeze. Even the priests were silenced.

For a long while the centurion sat on a rock and stared at the three silhouetted figures. Their heads were limp, occasionally rolling from side to side. The jeering was silent . . . eerily silent. Those who had wept, now waited.

Suddenly the center head ceased to bob. It yanked itself erect. Its eyes opened in a flash of white. A roar sliced the silence. "It is finished" (JOHN 19:30 NIV). It wasn't a yell. It wasn't a scream. It was a roar . . . a lion's roar. From what world that roar came the centurion didn't know, but he knew it wasn't this one.

The centurion stood up from the rock and took a few paces toward the Nazarene. As he got closer, he could tell that Jesus was staring into the sky. There was something in his eyes that the soldier had to see. But after only a few steps, he fell. He stood and fell again. The ground was shaking, gently at first and now violently. He tried once more to walk and was able to take a few steps and then fall . . . at the foot of the cross.

He looked up into the face of this one near death. The King looked down at the crusty old centurion. Jesus' hands were fastened; they couldn't reach out. His feet were nailed to timber; they couldn't walk toward him. His head was heavy with pain; he could scarcely move it. But his eyes . . . they were afire.

They were unquenchable. They were the eyes of God.

Perhaps that is what made the centurion say what he said. He saw the eyes of God. He saw the same eyes that had been seen by a near-naked adulteress in Jerusalem, a friendless divorcée in Samaria, and a four-day-dead Lazarus in a cemetery. The same eyes that didn't close upon seeing man's futility, didn't turn away at man's failure, and didn't wince upon witnessing man's death.

"It's all right," God's eyes said. "I've seen the storms and it's still all right."

The centurion's convictions began to flow together like rivers. "This was no carpenter," he spoke under his breath. "This was no peasant. This was no normal man."

He stood and looked around at the rocks that had fallen and the sky that had blackened. He turned and stared at the soldiers as they stared at Jesus with frozen faces. He turned and watched as the eyes of Jesus lifted and looked toward home. He listened as the parched lips parted and the swollen tongue spoke for the last time.

"Father, into your hands I commit my spirit" (LUKE 23:46 NIV).

Had the centurion not said it, the soldiers would have. Had the centurion not said it, the rocks would have—as would have the angels, the stars, even the demons. But he did say it. It fell to a nameless foreigner to state what they all knew.

"Surely he was the Son of God" (MATTHEW 27:54 NIV).

It was not the soldiers who killed him,

nor the screams of the mob:

It was his devotion to us.

Six hours, one Friday.

To the casual observer the six hours are mundane.
A shepherd with his sheep, a housewife with her thoughts,
a doctor with his patients. But to the handful of awestruck witnesses,
the most maddening of miracles is occurring.

God is on a cross. The creator of the universe is being executed.

Spit and blood are caked to his cheeks,
and his lips are cracked and swollen. Thorns rip his scalp.
His lungs scream with pain. His legs knot with cramps.
Taut nerves threaten to snap as pain twangs her morbid melody. . . .
And there is no one to save him, for he is sacrificing himself.

It is no normal six hours. . . .
it is no normal Friday.

SIX HOURS ONE FRIDAY

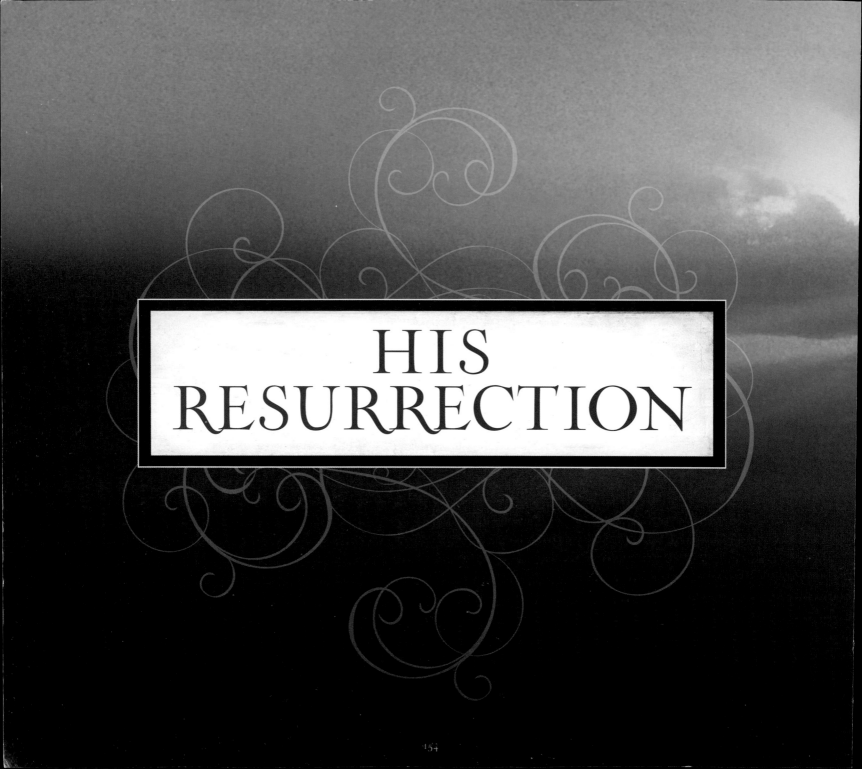

HIS
RESURRECTION

Jesus...

the moment he
removed the stone,
he removed all reason
for doubt.

CHRIST'S RESURRECTION

is an exploding flare

announcing to all sincere seekers

that it is

SAFE TO BELIEVE.

"Later, Joseph from Arimathea asked Pilate if he could take the body of Jesus.
(Joseph was a secret follower of Jesus, because he was afraid of the Jews.)
Pilate gave his permission, so Joseph came and took Jesus' body away. Nicodemus,
who earlier had come to Jesus at night, went with Joseph. He brought about seventy-five
pounds of myrrh and aloes. These two men took Jesus' body and wrapped it
with the spices in pieces of linen cloth, which is how the Jewish people bury the dead.
In the place where Jesus was crucified, there was a garden. In the garden was a
new tomb that had never been used before.

JOHN 19:38–41 NCV

RELUCTANT DURING CHRIST'S LIFE but courageous at his death, Joseph and Nicodemus came to serve Jesus. They came to bury him. They ascended the hill bearing the burial clothing.

Pilate had given his permission.

Joseph of Arimathea had given a tomb.

Nicodemus had brought the spices and linens.

John states that Nicodemus brought seventy-five pounds of myrrh and aloes. The amount is worth noting, for such a quantity of burial ointments was typically used only for kings.

He Chose the Nails

THE SEAL ON THE TOMB

To protect a letter, you seal the envelope. To keep air out of a jar, you seal its mouth with a rubber-ringed lid. To keep oxygen from the wine, you seal the opening with cork and wax. To seal a deal, you might sign a contract or notarize a signature. Sealing declares ownership and secures contents.

The most famous New Testament "sealing" occurred with the tomb of Jesus. Roman soldiers rolled a rock over the entrance and "set a seal on the stone" (MATTHEW 27:66 NASB). Archaeologists envision two ribbons stretched in front of the entrance, glued together with hardened wax that bore the imprimatur of the Roman government—SPQR *(Senatus Populusque Romanus)*—as if to say, "Stay away! The contents of this tomb belong to Rome."

Their seal, of course, proved futile.

COME THIRSTY

JESUS' BURIAL

WHEN PILATE LEARNED that Jesus was dead, he asked the soldier if they were certain. They were. Had they seen the Nazarene twitch, had they heard even one moan, they would have broken his legs to speed his end. But there was no need. The thrust of a spear removed all doubt. The Romans knew their job. And their job was finished. They pried loose the nails, lowered his body, and gave it to Joseph and Nicodemus.

Joseph of Arimathea. Nicodemus the Pharisee. They sat in seats of power and bore positions of influence. Men of means and men of clout. But they would've traded it all for one breath out of the body of Jesus. He had answered the prayer of their hearts, the prayer for the Messiah. As much as the soldiers wanted him dead, even more these men wanted him alive.

As they sponged the blood from his beard, don't you know they listened for his breath? As they wrapped the cloth around his hands, don't you know they hoped for a pulse? Don't you know they searched for life?

But they didn't find it.

So they do with him what they were expected to do with a dead man. They wrap his body in clean linen and place it in a tomb. Joseph's tomb. Roman guards are stationed to guard the corpse. And a Roman seal is set on the rock of the tomb. For three days, no one gets close to the grave.

But then, Sunday arrives. And with Sunday comes light—a light within the tomb. A bright light? A soft light? Flashing? Hovering? We don't know. But there was a light. For he is the light. And with the light came life. Just as the darkness was banished, now the decay is reversed. Heaven blows and Jesus breathes. His chest expands. Waxy lips open. Wooden fingers lift. Heart valves swish and hinged joints bend.

And, as we envision the moment, we stand in awe.

We stand in awe not just because of what we see, but because of what we know. . . . "We know that when Jesus was raised from the dead it was a signal of the end of death-as-the-end. Never again will death have the last word. When Jesus died, he took sin down with him, but alive he brings God down to us" (ROMANS 6:5–7 MSG).

BUT THEN, SUNDAY ARRIVES.

GOD LIVES TO HEAR YOUR HEARTBEAT.

He loves to hear your prayers.

HE'D DIE FOR YOUR SIN

BEFORE HE'D LET YOU DIE IN YOUR SIN,

so he did.

JOHN STAYED CLOSE BY

COULD THERE HAVE BEEN a greater tragedy for John than a dead Jesus? Three years earlier John had turned his back on his career and cast his lot with this Nazarene carpenter. Earlier in the week John had enjoyed a ticker-tape parade as Jesus and the disciples entered Jerusalem. Oh, how quickly things had turned! The people who had called him king on Sunday called for his death the following Friday. These linens were a tangible reminder that his friend and his future were wrapped in cloth and sealed behind a rock.

John didn't know on that Friday what you and I now know. He didn't know that Friday's tragedy would be Sunday's triumph. John would later confess that he "did not yet understand from the Scriptures that Jesus must rise from the dead" (JOHN 20:9 NCV).

THAT'S WHY WHAT HE DID ON SATURDAY IS SO IMPORTANT.

We don't know anything about this day; we have no passage to read, no knowledge to share. All we know is this: When Sunday came, John was still present. When Mary Magdalene came looking for him, she found him.

Jesus was dead. The Master's body was lifeless. John's friend and future were buried. But John had not left. Why? Was he waiting for the resurrection? No. As far as he knew, the lips were forever silent and the hands forever still. He wasn't expecting a Sunday surprise. Then why was he here?

You'd think he would have left. Who was to say that the men who crucified Christ wouldn't come after him? The crowds were pleased with one crucifixion; the religious leaders might have called for more. Why didn't John get out of town?

Perhaps the answer was pragmatic; perhaps he was taking care of Jesus' mother.

Or perhaps he didn't have anywhere else to go. Could be he didn't have any money or energy or direction . . . or all of the above.

Or maybe he lingered because he loved Jesus.

To others, Jesus was a miracle worker. To others, Jesus was a master teacher. To others, Jesus was the hope of Israel. But to John, he was all of these and more. To John, Jesus was a friend.

You don't abandon a friend—not even when that friend is dead. John stayed close to Jesus.

He had a habit of doing this. He was close to Jesus in the Upper Room. He was close to Jesus in the Garden of Gethsemane. He was at the foot of the cross at the crucifixion, and he was a quick walk from the tomb at the burial.

Did he understand Jesus? No.

Was he glad Jesus did what he did? No.

But did he leave Jesus? No.

We forget that

IMPOSSIBLE

is one of God's favorite words.

Mary Magdalene at Jesus' Tomb

A party was the last thing Mary Magdalene expected as she approached the tomb on that Sunday morning. The last few days had brought nothing to celebrate. The Jews could celebrate—Jesus was out of the way. The soldiers could celebrate—their work was done. But Mary couldn't celebrate. To her the last few days had brought nothing but tragedy.

MARY HAD BEEN THERE. She had heard the leaders clamor for Jesus' blood. She had witnessed the Roman whip rip the skin off his back. She had winced as the thorns sliced his brow and wept at the weight of the cross.

In the Louvre there is a painting of the scene of the cross. In the painting the stars are dead and the world is wrapped in darkness. In the shadows there is a kneeling form. It is Mary. She is holding her hands and lips against the bleeding feet of the Christ.

We don't know if Mary did that, but we know she could have. She was there. She was there to hold her arm around the shoulder of Mary the mother of Jesus. She was there to close his eyes. She was there.

So it's not surprising that she wants to be there again.

In the early morning mist she arises from her mat, takes her spices and aloes, and leaves her house, past the Gate of Gennath and up to the hillside. She anticipates a somber task. By now the body will be swollen. His face will be white. Death's odor will be pungent.

A gray sky gives way to gold as she walks up the narrow trail. As she rounds the final bend, she gasps. The rock in front of the grave is pushed back.

"Someone took the body." She runs to awaken Peter and John. They rush to see for themselves. She tries to keep up with them but can't.

Peter comes out of the tomb bewildered and John comes out believing, but Mary just sits in front of it weeping. The two men go home and leave her alone with her grief.

But something tells her she is not alone. Maybe she hears a noise. Maybe she hears a whisper. Or maybe she just hears her own heart tell her to take a look for herself.

Whatever the reason, she does. She stoops down, sticks her head into the hewn entrance, and waits for her eyes to adjust to the dark.

"Why are you crying?" She sees what looks to be a man, but he's white—radiantly white. He is one of two lights on either end of the vacant slab. Two candles blazing on an altar.

"Why are you crying?" An uncommon question to be asked in a cemetery. In fact, the question is rude. That is, unless the questioner knows something the questionee doesn't.

"They have taken my Lord away, and I don't know where they have put him."

She still calls him "my Lord." As far as she knows his lips were silent. As far as she knows, his corpse had been carted off by grave robbers. But in spite of it all, he is still her Lord.

Such devotion moves Jesus. It moves him closer to her. So close she hears him breathing. She turns and there he stands. She thinks he is the gardener.

Now, Jesus could have revealed himself at this point. He could have called for an angel to present him or a band to announce his presence. But he didn't.

"Why are you crying? Who is it you are looking for?" (JOHN 20:1–18 NIV).

He doesn't leave her wondering long, just long enough to remind us that he loves to surprise us. He waits for us to despair of human strength and then intervenes with heavenly. God waits for us to give up and then—surprise!

And listen to the surprise as Mary's name is spoken by a man she loved—a man she had buried.

"Miriam."

God appearing at the strangest of places. Doing the strangest of things. Stretching smiles where there had hung only frowns. Placing twinkles where there were only tears. Hanging a bright star in a dark sky. Arching rainbows in the midst of thunderclouds. Calling names in a cemetery.

"Miriam," he said softly, "surprise!"

Mary was shocked. It's not often you hear your name spoken by an eternal tongue. But when she did, she recognized it. And when she did, she responded correctly. She worshiped him.

Six Hours One Friday

WHO IS IT YOU ARE LOOKING FOR?

Jesus

His Resurrected Body

Jesus appeared to the followers in a flesh-and-bone body: "A spirit does not have flesh and bones as you see that I have" (LUKE 24:39 NASB). His resurrected body was a real body, real enough to walk on the road to Emmaus, to be mistaken for that of a gardener, to swallow fish at breakfast. ❋ In the same breath, Jesus' real body was really different. The Emmaus disciples didn't recognize him, and walls didn't stop him. Mark tried to describe the new look and settled for "[Jesus] appeared in another form" (MARK 16:12 NKJV). While his body was the same, it was better; it was glorified. It was a heavenly body. ❋ And I can't find the passage that says he shed it. He ascended in it. "He was lifted up while they were looking on, and a cloud received Him out of their sight" (ACTS 1:9 NASB). He will return in it. The angel told the followers, "This Jesus, who has been taken up from you into heaven, will come in just the same way as you have watched Him go into heaven" (ACTS 1:11 NASB). ❋ The God-man is still both. The hands that blessed the bread of the boy now bless the prayers of the millions. And the mouth that commissions angels is the mouth that kissed children. ❋ You know what this means? The greatest force in the cosmos understands and intercedes for you. "We have an Advocate with the Father, Jesus Christ the righteous" (1 JOHN 2:1 NASB).

NEXT DOOR SAVIOR

HE LOVES WITH AN

unfailing love.

Peter's Breakfast with Jesus

SEE THE FELLOW in the shadows? That's Peter. Peter the apostle. Peter the impetuous. Peter the passionate. He once walked on water. Stepped right out of the boat onto the lake. He'll soon preach to thousands. Fearless before friends and foes alike. But tonight the one who stepped on the water has hurried into hiding. The one who will speak with power is weeping in pain.

Not sniffling or whimpering, but weeping. Bawling. Bearded face buried in thick hands. His howl echoing in the Jerusalem night. What hurts more? The fact that he did it? Or the fact that he swore he never would?

"Lord, I am ready to go with you to prison and even to die with you!" he pledged only hours earlier. "But Jesus said, 'Peter, before the rooster crows this day, you will say three times that you don't know me'" (LUKE 22:33–34 NCV).

Denying Christ on the night of his betrayal was bad enough, but did he have to boast that he wouldn't? And one denial was pitiful, but three? Three denials were horrific, but did he have to curse? "Peter began to place a curse on himself and swear, 'I don't know the man'" (MATTHEW 26:74 NCV).

And now, awash in a whirlpool of sorrow, Peter is hiding. Peter is weeping. And soon Peter will be fishing.

We wonder why he goes fishing. We know why he goes to Galilee. He had been told that the risen Christ would meet the disciples there. The arranged meeting place is not the sea, however, but a mountain (MATTHEW 28:16). If the followers were to meet Jesus on a mountain, what are they doing in a boat? No one told them to fish, but that's what they did. "Simon Peter said, 'I am going out to fish.' The others said, 'We will go with you'" (JOHN 21:3 NCV). Besides, didn't Peter quit fishing? Two years earlier, when Jesus called him to fish for men, didn't he drop his net and follow? We haven't seen him fish since. We never see him fish again. Why is he fishing now? Especially now! Jesus has risen from the dead. Peter has seen the empty tomb. Who could fish at a time like this?

Were they hungry? Perhaps that's the sum of it. Maybe the expedition was born out of growling stomachs.

Or then again, maybe it was born out of a broken heart.

You see, Peter could not deny his denial. The empty tomb did not erase the crowing rooster. Christ had returned, but Peter wondered, he must have wondered, "After what I did, would he return for someone like me?"

We've wondered the same. Is Peter the only person to do the very thing he swore he'd never do?

"Infidelity is behind me!"

"From now on, I'm going to bridle my tongue."

"No more shady deals. I've learned my lesson."

Oh, the volume of our boasting. And, oh, the heartbreak of our shame.

Rather than resist the flirting, we return it.

Rather than ignore the gossip, we share it.

Rather than stick to the truth, we shade it.

And the rooster crows, and conviction pierces, and Peter has a partner in the shadows. We weep as Peter wept, and we do what Peter did. We go fishing. We go back to our old lives. We return to our pre-Jesus practices. We do what comes naturally, rather than what comes spiritually. And we question whether Jesus has a place for folks like us.

Jesus answers that question. He answers it for you and me and all who tend to "Peter out" on Christ. His answer came on the shore of the sea in a gift to Peter. You know what Jesus did? Split the waters? Turn the boat to gold and the nets to silver? No, Jesus did something much more meaningful. He invited Peter to breakfast. Jesus prepared a meal.

Of course, the breakfast was one special moment among several that morning. There was the great catch of fish and the recognition of Jesus. The plunge of Peter and the paddling of the disciples. And there was the moment they reached the shore and found Jesus next to a fire of coals. The fish were sizzling, and the bread was waiting, and the defeater of hell and the ruler of heaven invited his friends to sit down and have a bite to eat.

No one could have been more grateful than Peter.

The idea that a virgin would be selected by God to bear himself. . . .
The notion that God would don a scalp and toes and two eyes. . . .
The thought that the King of the universe would sneeze and
burp and get bit by mosquitoes. . . .
It's too incredible. Too revolutionary.
We would never create such a Savior.
We aren't that daring. . . .

In our wildest imaginings we wouldn't conjure
a king who becomes one of us.

But God did. God did what we wouldn't dare dream.
He did what we couldn't imagine.
He became a man so we could trust him.
He became a sacrifice so we could know him.
And he defeated death so we could follow him.

AND THE ANGELS WERE SILENT

175

HIS LEGACY

Jesus...

those who saw him

were never the same.

Christ came to earth for one reason:

to give his life as a ransom for you,

for me,

FOR ALL OF US.

HE SACRIFICED HIMSELF
TO GIVE US
A SECOND CHANCE.

He Did It Just for You

WHEN GOD ENTERED TIME and became a man, he who was boundless became bound. Imprisoned in flesh. Restricted by weary-prone muscles and eyelids. For more than three decades, his once limitless reach would be limited to the stretch of an arm, his speed checked to the pace of human feet.

I wonder, was he ever tempted to reclaim his boundlessness? In the middle of a long trip, did he ever consider transporting himself to the next city? When the rain chilled his bones, was he tempted to change the weather? When the heat parched his lips, did he give thought to popping over to the Caribbean for some refreshment?

If ever he entertained such thoughts, he never gave in to them. Not once. Stop and think about this. Not once did Christ use his supernatural powers for personal comfort. With one word he could've transformed the hard earth into a soft bed, but he didn't. With a wave of his hand, he could've boomeranged the spit of his accusers back into their faces, but he didn't. With an arch of his brow, he could've paralyzed the hand of the soldier as he braided the crown of thorns. But he didn't.

Want to know the coolest thing about the coming?

Not that the One who played marbles with the stars gave it up to play marbles with marbles. Or that the One who hung the galaxies gave it up to hang door-jambs to the displeasure of a cranky client who wanted everything yesterday but couldn't pay for anything until tomorrow.

Not that he, in an instant, went from needing nothing to needing air, food, a tub of hot water and salts for his tired feet, and, more than anything, needing somebody—anybody—who was more concerned about where he would spend eternity than where he would spend Friday's paycheck.

Or that he resisted the urge to fry the two-bit, self-appointed hall monitors of holiness who dared suggest that he was doing the work of the devil.

Not that he kept his cool while the dozen best friends he ever had felt the heat and got out of the kitchen. Or that he gave no command to the angels who begged, "Just give the nod, Lord. One word and these demons will be deviled eggs."

Not that he refused to defend himself when blamed for every sin of every slut and sailor since Adam. Or that he stood silent as a million guilty verdicts echoed in the tribunal of heaven and the giver of light was left in the chill of a sinner's night.

Not even that after three days in a dark hole he stepped into the Easter sunrise with a smile and a swagger and a question for lowly Lucifer—"Is that your best punch?"

That was cool, incredibly cool.

But want to know the coolest thing about the One who gave up the crown of heaven for a crown of thorns?

He did it for you. *Just for you.*

Jesus says

HE IS THE SOLUTION

for weariness of soul.

His Goodness and Mercy

Dare we envision a God who follows us? Who follows us with "goodness and mercy" all the days of our lives? ✳ The disciples of Jesus knew the feeling of being followed by God. They were rain soaked and shivering when they looked over their shoulders and saw Jesus walking toward them. God had followed them into the storm. ✳ An unnamed Samaritan woman knew the same. She was alone in life and alone at the well when she looked over her shoulder and heard a Messiah speaking. God had followed her through her pain. ✳ John the Apostle was banished on Patmos when he looked over his shoulder and saw the skies begin to open. God had followed him into his exile. ✳ Lazarus was three days dead in a sealed tomb when he heard a voice, lifted his head, and looked over his shoulder and saw Jesus standing. God had followed him into death. ✳ Peter had denied his Lord and gone back to fishing when he heard his name and looked over his shoulder and saw Jesus cooking breakfast. God had followed him in spite of his failure. ✳ God is the God who follows. I wonder . . . have you sensed him following you? Still he follows. Never forcing us. Never leaving us. Patiently persistent. Faithfully present. Using all of his power to convince us that he is who he is and that he can be trusted to lead us home. ✳ His goodness and mercy will follow us all the days of our lives.

Traveling Light

THE MOVEMENT CONTINUES

The belief of French philosopher Voltaire: The Bible and Christianity would pass within a hundred years.
He died in 1778;
The movement continues.

The pronouncement of Friedrich Nietzsche in 1882: "God is dead."
The dawn of science, he believed, would be the doom of faith.
Science has dawned;
the movement continues.

The way a Communist dictionary defined the Bible: "It is a collection of fantastic legends without any scientific support."
Communism is diminishing;
the movement continues.

THE DISCOVERY made by every person who has tried to bury the faith. The same as the one made by those who tried to bury its Founder: He won't stay in the tomb.

The facts. The movement has never been stronger. Over one billion Catholics and nearly as many Protestants.

The question. How do we explain it? Jesus was a backwater peasant. He never wrote a book, never held an office. He never journeyed more than two hundred miles from his hometown. Friends left him. One betrayed him. Those he helped forgot him. Prior to his death they abandoned him. But after his death they couldn't resist him. What made the difference?

The answer. His death and resurrection. For when he died, so did your sin. And when he rose, so did your hope. For when he rose, your grave was changed from a final residence to temporary housing.

The reason he did it. The face in your mirror.

The verdict after two millenniums. Herod was right: There is room for only one King.

He Is Love

"Love . . . endures all things" (1 CORINTHIANS 13:4–7 NASB).

He could have given up. No one would have known otherwise. Jesus could have given up.

One look at the womb could have discouraged him. God is as unbridled as the air and limitless as the sky. Would he reduce his world to the belly of a girl for nine months?

And nine months? There is another reason to quit. Heaven has no months. Heaven has no time. Or, perhaps better said, heaven has all the time. It's we who are running out. Ours passes so quickly that we measure it by the second. Wouldn't Christ rather stay on the other side of the ridge of time?

He could have. He could have given up. If not, at least he could have stopped short. Did he have to become flesh? How about becoming light? Here is an idea. Heaven could open, and Christ could fall on the earth in the form of a white light. And then in the light there could be a voice, a booming, thundering, teeth-shaking voice. Toss in a gust of wind and the angels for background vocals, and the whole world notices!

As things turned out, when he came, hardly anyone noticed. Bethlehem held no parade. The village offered no banquet. You'd think a holiday would have been appropriate. At least a few streamers for the stable.

And the stable. Is that not yet another reason for Christ to back out? Stables are smelly, dirty. Stables have no linoleum floors or oxygen tanks. How are they going to cut the umbilical cord? And who is going to cut the umbilical cord? Joseph? A small-time carpenter from a one-camel town? Is there not a better father for God? Someone with an education, a pedigree. Someone with a bit of clout? This fellow couldn't even swing a room at the hotel. You think he's got what it takes to be the father to the Maker of the universe?

Jesus could have given up. Imagine the change he had to make, the distance he had to travel. What would it be like to become flesh? . . .

Love goes the distance . . . and Christ traveled from limitless eternity to be confined by time in order to become one of us. He didn't have to. He could have given up. At any step along the way he could have called it quits.

When he saw the size of the womb, he could have stopped.

When he saw how tiny his hand would be, how soft his voice would be, how hungry his tummy would be, he could have stopped. At the first whiff of the stinky stable, at the first gust of cold air. The first time he scraped his knee or blew his nose or tasted burnt bagels, he could have turned and walked out.

When he saw the dirt floor of his Nazareth house. When Joseph gave him a chore to do. When his fellow students were dozing off during the reading of the Torah, his Torah. When the neighbor took his name in vain. When the lazy farmer blamed his poor crop on God. At any point Jesus could have said, "That's it! That's enough! I'm going home." But he didn't.

He didn't, because he is love. And "love . . . endures all things" (1 CORINTHIANS 13:4–7 NKJV).

A LOVE WORTH GIVING

Jesus LOVE GOES THE DISTANCE

HE WAS GOD-MAN.

Jesus was not a godlike man, nor a manlike God. He was God-man.

Midwifed by a carpenter.

Bathed by a peasant girl.

The maker of the world with a bellybutton.

The author of the Torah being taught the Torah.

Heaven's human. And because he was, we are left with scratch-your-head, double-blink, what's-wrong-with-this-picture? moments like these:

Bordeaux instead of H2O.

A cripple sponsoring the town dance.

A sack lunch satisfying five thousand tummies.

And, most of all, a grave: guarded by soldiers, sealed by a rock, yet vacated by a three-days-dead man.

What do we do with such moments?

What do we do with such a person? We applaud men for doing good things. We enshrine God for doing great things. But when a man does God things?

One thing is certain, we can't ignore him.

NEXT DOOR SAVIOR

HE INVITES US TO LOVE HIM.

HE URGES US TO LOVE HIM.

But, in the end, the choice is yours and mine.

HIS NAME IS

Jesus

SOURCES

All of the material in this book was originally published in the following books by Max Lucado. All copyrights to the original works are held by the author, Max Lucado.

The Applause of Heaven (Nashville: Thomas Nelson, Inc., 1990).

In the Eye of the Storm (Nashville: Thomas Nelson, Inc., 1991).

He Still Moves Stones (Nashville: Thomas Nelson, Inc., 1993).

When God Whispers Your Name (Nashville: Thomas Nelson, Inc., 1994).

A Gentle Thunder (Nashville: Thomas Nelson, Inc., 1995).

The Great House of God (Nashville: Thomas Nelson, Inc., 1997).

Just Like Jesus (Nashville: Thomas Nelson, Inc., 1998).

When Christ Comes (Nashville: Thomas Nelson, Inc., 1999).

Traveling Light (Nashville: Thomas Nelson, Inc., 2000).

He Chose the Nails (Nashville: Thomas Nelson, Inc., 2000).

A Love Worth Giving (Nashville: Thomas Nelson, Inc., 2002).

And the Angels Were Silent (Nashville: Thomas Nelson, Inc., 2003).

God Came Near (Nashville: Thomas Nelson, Inc., 2003).

Next Door Savior (Nashville: Thomas Nelson, Inc., 2003).

No Wonder They Call Him the Savior (Nashville: Thomas Nelson, Inc., 2003).

Six Hours One Friday (Nashville: Thomas Nelson, Inc., 2003).

Come Thirsty (Nashville: Thomas Nelson, Inc., 2004).

It's Not About Me (Nashville: Thomas Nelson, Inc., 2004).

Cure for the Common Life (Nashville: Thomas Nelson, Inc., 2005).

Every Day Deserves a Chance (Nashville: Thomas Nelson, Inc., 2007).